BOMBS &
BETTY
GRABLE

JOHN
WILCOX

BREWIN BOOKS

First published by
Brewin Books Ltd, 56 Alcester Road,
Studley, Warwickshire B80 7LG in 2010
www.brewinbooks.com

ISBN: 978–1–85858–456–0

A Cataloguing in Publication Record
for this title is available from the British Library.

Typeset in Bembo
Printed in Great Britain by
Hobbs the Printers Ltd.

FSC
Mixed Sources
Product group from well-managed
forests and other controlled sources
Cert no. SA-COC-1530
www.fsc.org
© 1996 Forest Stewardship Council

CONTENTS

Acknowledgements   vi
Foreword   viii

PART I. BOMBS AND BETTY GRABLE   1

1.   Alfred The Great   2
2.   "You Don't Hear The One That Gets You"   12
3.   Yes, We Have No Bananas…   24
4.   "The Best Governed City In The World"   29
5.   "The Second Casualty Of War"   37
6.   Moon Over Miami   45
7.   "A Mighty Lighthouse Of Knowledge"   54
8.   Relationships: "The Friendly Invasion"   61
9.   Friendship   69
10.   The Good Or The Bad Old Days?   73

PART II. THE YEARS IN BETWEEN   79

11.   "Silly Little Sod"   80
12.   Bright Lights And Dark Mills   91

PART III. THE STORY OF PAUL   99

13.   The How Of It   100
14.   The Why Of It   107
15.   The End Of It   122

ACKNOWLEDGEMENTS

I am grateful to my sister, Margaret Wilkins, and to my cousins Elaine Read, Ramon Lloyd and Vincent Nicholls, for helping to prompt and sometimes supplement my memory of what happened all those years ago. My thanks also go to Martyn Bennett, Deputy Head of Aston Campus at Broadway School, Birmingham, and to Inge Thornton, Community Librarian at Aston Library, for sharing her affection for that old institution with me.

I gladly acknowledge Sainsburys as the source of many of the statistics and facts I used about wartime rationing in Chapter 3 and, while my own memory and interpretations were the main source of the material used throughout the book, I frequently took refuge in books of and about the period. In this context, the London Library, as ever, was most helpful. I must also record my gratitude to my agent, Jane Conway-Gordon, for her support and to my publisher, Alan Brewin, for his suggestions for changes to the text and his son, Alistair, for his work on layout and picture research.

The following publications were particularly useful to me in terms of background reading:

Victorian Cities by Asa Briggs (Odhams Press, 1963);
Victorian and Edwardian Birmingham by Dorothy McCulla (B.T. Batsford, 1973);
The Public Library in Britain 1914–2000 by Alistair Black (The British Library, 2000);
Library and Community by K.C. Harrison (Andre Deutsch Ltd, 1963);
The New Biographical Dictionary of Film by David Thomson (Little Brown, 2002):
The War, the West and the Wilderness by Kevin Brownlow (Secker and Warburg, 1978).

THE STORY OF PAUL.
I give my love and thanks to my wife Betty and daughter Alison for their help in recollecting the details recalled in this part of my story. I must also record my gratitude for the comments on this part of the draft manuscript given by two old friends –

although not *that* old, for they never knew Paul – Jim Farrand and, in particular, his partner, Sharon Jury, a (good) Samaritan with a down to earth knowledge of working with would-be and actual suicides.

The books I mention in the narrative are:

The Outsider by Albert Camus (Penguin Books, London, 1961);
The Myth of Sisyphus by Albert Camus (Penguin Books, London 1977);
The Savage God by A. Alvarez (Penguin Books, London, 1979);
Why People Die of Suicide by Thomas Joiner (Harvard University Press, Cambridge Massachusetts and London 2005).

FOREWORD

This book is not intended to be a conventional autobiography and not even really a memoir. It is more a recording of two halves of a life, discrete and even self-contained recollections of different happenings in the beginning of my life and at some way towards its end, with a brief narrative in the middle to link the two. In many respects the two may appeal to a different readership: those who are interested in or who themselves recollect what it was like to grow up in a large industrial city, targeted by German bombers in World War II; and those who are intrigued by the possibility of life after death and one family's experience of it, however vicarious. The link between the two, of course, is me. I hope, immodestly, that this and the straightforward telling of what happened to me in between is sufficient to bind the two stories together.

JW
Chilmark, June 2009

Part I

BOMBS AND BETTY GRABLE

Chapter 1

ALFRED THE GREAT

Let's start with Uncle Alf, although we shouldn't because the early part of this book is the story of a boy growing up during the years of World War II and Alfred Wilcox was very much a man of World War I. Yet he did loom large throughout my childhood and he returned to dominate nine months of my later life, like some spectre released from a dusty bottle found in an attic. Having said that, looming is not something Alf did, in that he was not a large, physically dominating man. In fact, he was of medium height and build, good looking as I remember him in middle and old age, in a red-faced, fleshy kind of way, with wavy hair and bright eyes twinkling above his pipe and a jaw that was square and redolent of Empire. He was jolly and forceful in conversation and, when he spoke, everyone listened to him. Whether this was because of respect for what he had done or the wisdom of his observation I don't know. I was too young to tell the difference. I only knew that Uncle Alf was famous and, in effect, the leader of my father's family.

Originally, there were fourteen of them, seven boys and seven girls, all born over a period of twenty eight years, stretching from Uncle John, in 1874, to 1902, when Aunt Ada was produced as the last of the litter. That means that my paternal grandmother, Sarahann, had her first child at the age of nineteen and the last at forty seven, regularly giving birth every two years. I never met her, of course, and I do not know when she died but one can't help feeling that the poor soul could not have lasted much beyond the birth of that fourteenth child. All the children were born and brought up in the back streets of Birmingham, as was I, many years later, leaving me with the conviction that Birmingham, in fact, never had any front streets at all.

The census of 1881 has eight of the family, including Sarahann's 20-year-old brother, living in a back-to-back house behind 40, Wilton Street, Aston. It is unlikely that that kind of accommodation would provide more than two bedrooms, so the sleeping arrangements must have been cosy, to say the least. Alf arrived three years later to add to the congestion. He was the middle one in the roll call of infants, born on 16th December 1884, at a time when William Ewart Gladstone was steering the third reform Bill through the British parliament and the country was waiting to hear if Gordon had been relieved at Khartoum (he had not). My father, Leonard Wilcox, was the last of the boys to arrive, in 1893, and only three sisters were younger. As a result, I remember none of my uncles and aunts older than Alf and that, I suppose, helps to give him the patriarchal image that I retain of him. Although what he was to do at the age of 33 was enough to thrust him forward as an iconic figure to me anyway.

All of the seven brothers enlisted to fight the Germans in the war of 1914–18. Each one became a rifle and bayonet man, fighting in the trenches, serving in a surprisingly wide spread of infantry regiments. Amazingly, they all survived the carnage to return to their homes in Aston, within a cheer of Villa Park, the home of Aston Villa, then arguably the most famous football club in the world. If a twist of fate had allowed them to be born a little higher up the social scale, so that perhaps they would have been sent to public school and even university, then surely they would have perished in the mud as subalterns, like so many others, leading their men with whistle and revolver, to be picked off by the German snipers. As it was, as rankers, they returned laden with honours – and wounds.

Bernard, born in 1889, became a sergeant, was awarded the Military Medal, but lost an eye. Leonard, my father, also gained three stripes and went over the top at the Somme, to be hit by shell fire which riddled his lungs with shrapnel, so causing consumption and a lingering death in 1945. Ernest, slim and perky, born in 1892, became a temporary Regimental Sergeant Major at the ridiculously young age of nineteen, "because there was nobody else left." He came back with the Distinguished Conduct Medal, the second highest award for bravery. It was Alfred, however, who was to become the family leader, yet strangely only a Lance Corporal then, who won the Victoria Cross, Britain's highest decoration for valour.

It earned him, of course, undying fame throughout his life. Why, it was even whispered that he had had *two* separate conversations with the Prince of Wales (later to become, briefly, King Edward VIII and, interminably, the Duke of Windsor)! It is true that the First World War produced 628 awards of the V.C., compared to 128 in the Second World War, so fierce and close was the fighting and consequently so much greater the opportunities for displaying extreme courage. But, even so, the qualities necessary to earn the award are so demanding that the distinction then, as now, remained enduring.

Alfred earned his glory in less than an hour – perhaps only forty five minutes or so – of desperate hand-to-hand fighting on 12th September 1918, only days, in fact, before the end of hostilities. He was serving with the 2/4th Oxford and Buckinghamshire Light Infantry near Laventie, France, when his company was held up by heavy fire at short range from a nest of four German machine guns. His citation for the cross describes the ensuing action like this:

"L/Cpl Wilcox rushed to the nearest enemy gun, bombing it and killing the gunner. Being then attacked by an enemy bombing party, he picked up enemy stick bombs and led his company against the next gun, finally capturing and destroying it. Then, left with only one man, he continued bombing and captured a third gun. Going up the trench, bombing as he went, he captured a fourth gun and then returned to his platoon."

In fact, like all citations, it does not tell the whole story and it is incorrect in some detail (Alf did not "lead his company," for instance, he had only a section of three men with him). Alfred himself told it more comprehensively and certainly more graphically when he addressed a regimental gathering of the 2/1st Royal Bucks Hussars (the regiment in which he had served before transferring to the Ox and Bucks LI) in Birmingham's Cannon Street Hotel on 7th May 1920.

"My battalion," he said, "was ordered to take what was known as Junction Post, believed to be strongly held by machine guns. I was in charge of the leading section and my duty was to cut through the wire and locate the posts. Having got to the wire and successfully cut it, I went back for my section, which I had left in a shell hole a hundred yards in the rear, only to find all but one wounded. That one I told to follow me. Getting through the gap I had already cut and making my way to the trench the enemy was holding, I got into it and proceeded up the trench and, bombing my way, I captured my first gun. I continued up the trench, capturing a second gun after a hand to hand struggle in which I bayoneted my man; then bombing a third post, killing five. My own rifle this time being clogged with mud, I had to resort to German stick bombs, which accounted for a fourth post with its gun. I carried on, driving the remainder of the post away, leaving behind them about twelve dead in all and four guns – one light, three heavy. I then returned to the guns. Finding I could not remove the three heavies, I put them out of action and had to withdraw owing to lack of support and no fire-arms, my own gun having been dumped for the free use of German stick bombs."

Seven weeks later, Alf took part in the attack on St Hubert and received a bullet through the ankle, resulting in him being discharged early in 1919. I have still a photograph of him – a full Corporal by now – flanked by a female nurse and a woman doctor, standing one legged on crutches in his hospital "blues" and smiling half apologetically. Even in the most unpromising situations, Alfred could always attract the ladies.

He had married, in fact, in 1913 and had three children, Doris, Leonard and Douglas, and both boys served in the army in the Second World War. Alas, the marriage was not happy and Alf and his wife Louise separated in the late thirties. I remember overhearing my father confide to my mother at about this time that he had always felt that Alf "had gone a bit mad" on that September day in 1918 because his domestic unhappiness had given him no hope for the future (divorce, in those days, was not for working class people).

Even so, it was clear that Alfred's courage was endemic and not something induced by despair. My father recalled that when the circus came to the Serpentine Ground, just behind Aston Parish Church in the 1900's, it was the young Alf who was the only one in the audience under the Big Top to take up the lion tamer's challenge to crack a bottle of champagne with him inside the lion's cage. Years later, during World War II, when the hero was a publican in his sixties, he did not hesitate to vault his bar and knock down a drunken sailor who was being disparaging about the stammering King George VI.

It would be wrong, however, to attribute braggadocio to the man. I remember him for his joviality, not his swagger. He could be gruff occasionally to the collection of nephews and nieces that were allowed to play in the yards of the inner city pubs he managed in his declining years when their parents visited— and God knows I, for one, was always in awe of him. But he was always fundamentally kind and — the abiding memory — usually jolly, his beaming red cheeks a fine testimony to the ale he sold.

I was never encouraged to talk to my father about his own war experiences. During my early years, the tuberculosis that would eventually kill him was taking hold and adding bitterness to the despair he felt about the state of the post-war world. He did not wish, therefore, to re-visit his time in the mud and misery of what we all then called The Great War. It was even more unlikely, then, that I should approach Uncle Alfred to hear of his exploits at first hand. And, from talking now to those few who remember him, he was not given to speaking of them gratuitously. He did not dine out on them.

So I never did see the Cross. My younger cousin Ramon, however, did so. Because Alfred's marriage had broken down, he needed a woman to be his consort at the public house he kept and his young sister Lillian took her husband and two children to live with her brother and help him manage his house. Alfred's fame ensured that he always kept substantial pubs with more than adequate living accommodation provided above the bars. So it was that Ramon, Lillian's child, chanced one day upon his uncle carefully putting away his medals in the safe and, speaking with the courage of familiarity, asked to see the medal. The old man took the boy on his knee and allowed him to handle the famous bronze cross, still made in those days from the cannon captured from the Russians during the Crimean War. I always envied Ray that.

My famous uncle only turned to the licensed trade in his middle age. He had trained as a diamond mounter in Birmingham's famous jewellery quarter (it was almost inevitable that my father, his admiring younger brother, should follow in his footsteps in that craft) and he worked for a time, both before and after the war, in London's Hatton Garden. The depression, however, hit that luxury trade hard and both he and my father were put out of work in the early thirties. Alfred had a succession of jobs, including managing a quarry just outside Birmingham, before his local celebrity, like that of retired professional footballers in those days, earned him a series of tenancies of large public houses in the inner city.

His modest fame, of course, went with him and he was chairman of his local British Legion branch, both in London and Birmingham. His easy manner and celebrity made him a popular publican in those dark streets and my memory of visits to him with my parents as a boy during the war were of happy, booming laughter coming from crowded bars as my cousins and I played in the yard or upstairs in those high-ceiling, Victorian rooms and corridors.

My father and Alfred were close, despite the nine years' age gap between them. Alf was best man at his younger brother's wedding in 1921 and, in a pleasing piece of symmetry, he spoke at my own wedding in 1953. He wasn't scheduled to do so but my mother felt on the day that it would be an unforgivable act of *lèse majesté* for Alfred to attend a formal family function without addressing the gathering. So she leaned across to me and whispered "call on Alf to say a few words." As a result, the poor man was introduced without any warning or preparation and spoke off the cuff for all of four minutes. I can't remember the detail of what he said – though I certainly do recall cringing as the British Empire and bulwarks of it like my father were introduced – but it was effective and received the biggest round of applause of the day. I never saw him again. He died in March, the following year, at the age of 69.

The funeral didn't cause much of a stir. It was a time when veterans of the First World War were quietly slipping away and, of course, Alf's fame had receded anyway as new heroes had been created in the second war. Nevertheless, his old regiment sent a warrant officer and a bugler to do the honours and the Last Post sounded plaintively among the gravestones of Aston Church's cemetery. The cemetery is now closed to new graves and the fine old red-brick church, built on the site of an earlier Norman place of worship, now stands mutely under the roar of the awful Spaghetti Junction's concrete pillars. But the churchyard looked fine on that early spring day in 1954.

As a young reporter on the Birmingham Gazette I covered the story for my newspaper. I remember that those who were left of my uncles took pride in getting the visiting soldiers drunk after the ceremony. I also remember feeling pleased that Alf had been buried just about a hundred yards away from my father's grave, which rested a little higher up the gently sloping hill. That memory was to prove important fifty two years later.

It was the last time, I believe, that the remaining descendants of that large Victorian Wilcox family came together. A year later, I left to work in London and, when my mother and sister moved to the north west and then the west country, I rarely visited Birmingham. But my wife, Betty, and I chanced to be back there some fifteen years ago.

We took flowers to put on my father's grave (endearingly, someone had chalked "f★★k the Baggies" on the church wall near his head stone) and I walked down the hill to pay my respects to Uncle Alf. There was no sign of his grave. No headstone and no other indication that he was buried where I roughly remembered the grave to be. I tramped between the overgrown old graves but there was no clue to the the last resting place of one of Birmingham's few V.C.s. The cemetery seemed smaller somehow and I came to the conclusion that its bottom portion must have been bulldozed away to make way for an extension to the supermarket car park that stood on the site of the old circus ground. Uncle Alf, I presumed, must have gone with it. Indignant, I made a note of the Vicar's name and telephone number to ring him in protest. But life was short and, on returning south, I shamefully never got around to it.

But Alfred Wilcox, like the best of old soldiers, had a habit of not fading away. About eight years after my visit to the graveyard, I heard that his Victoria Cross had been sold. After his death, it had been inherited by his eldest son, Leonard, who alas had died only four years after his father. Leonard had had no children, so the cross therefore was passed on to Alf's younger son, Douglas, who himself died in 1996, leaving the medal in the care of his wife. She, I learned, had sold it to a dealer for an unknown figure and the dealer, in turn, had auctioned it in London for a sum said to be £55,000, £17,000 above the reserve price. Only someone extremely rich – certainly not the Regiment – would have paid that price and it ensued that the Cross had been added to the private collection of Lord Ashcroft, former treasurer of the Conservative Party and an avid accumulator of these precious medals.

Those of us left of the family who remembered Alf shook our heads in dismay and wished that we had been offered the chance to raise funds to buy the cross to present it to the regiment's museum in Oxford. Wishful thinking, almost certainly, for none of us possessed that kind of disposable wealth. But it would have been good to have had the opportunity, at least. Nevertheless, the sale of the medal did bring a belated bonus for the family.

When Alfred's marriage broke up his family split. The boys stayed with their father but the daughter, Doris, took her mother to live with her and her husband in various parts of the UK and had one daughter, Elaine. There had been little contact between the brothers and sister after Alf's death and Elaine had grown up longing to know more about her grandfather and her two uncles, not knowing that there was a much wider family. Divorced, with three grown up boys, she had never met Alfred but was living in Nottingham when she read about the sale of the Cross. Her local paper wrote about her desire to meet her relatives and a cutting of the story was sent to me. I contacted Elaine, a meeting was arranged and she subsequently became a dear and welcome addition to the family. As it turned out, she was not to be the last of Alf's hitherto unknown descendants to come in out of the cold, but more of that later.

We must fast forward now. By January 2006 I had gained a tiny smidgeon of fame myself as a novelist and had dedicated my first, non-fiction book, to the memory of my father and of his three brothers who had won their medals in World War I. As a result, my publishers received a request in that month from a local historian in Birmingham who was attempting to track down the last resting places of the city's holders of the Victoria Cross, to include in a book he was hoping to write about them. He had visited Aston Churchyard looking for Alfred Wilcox, but could find nothing. More to the point, the Church's record of burials covering the time of Alf's interment were strangely missing. Could I help him?

Intrigued, I drove to Birmingham and lunched with Christopher Sutton, the researcher. Together, we trudged through the churchyard, now looking considerably the worst for wear. Once again, I could find absolutely no trace of a headstone or grave where I remembered Alfred to be. The young Vicar, the Rev Andy Jolley, could provide no solution, either to the whereabouts of the grave or the missing records, except to assure me that no church ground had ever been sold or demolished. What's more, it ensued that Sutton and I were not the only people looking for my uncle. The Ox and Bucks Regimental Association, anxious to pin down the lasting resting place of one of their own, had searched too, as had other local historians and representatives of veteran associations.

Somehow, the news of our and their hunt had reached the local media and Alfred regained a little of his previous fame. To the newspapers, radio and TV my Uncle Alf had become "The Lost VC."

Why? How had his grave disappeared? Where was the headstone? Why had the records of burials during the two years covering his interment disappeared?

I set out to find answers to these questions and then to try and co-ordinate the efforts of those searching for Alf and to see if some kind of memorial could be erected to him, either at the spot where I remember him being buried or in Aston Parish Church itself. It became a nine-month mission.

I soon came to the reluctant conclusion that no headstone had ever been erected on Alfred's grave. For some reason, his two sons, whose responsibility this was, had not done so. Those close to them could offer no solution. There was no rift with their father, they were both in good jobs and could easily have afforded a good stone. Perhaps, it simply slipped their mind. Perhaps… The result, anyway, was that it was quite impossible to verify the exact location of the grave, although a combination of my own memory and that of my sister and cousins who had also been at the burial, produced a consensus of its approximate position.

The puzzle of the missing records had to remain a mystery. Neither the Acting Bishop of Birmingham nor the Rev Jolley could offer any explanation. It it seemed to be just an unhappy coincidence and I was forced to leave it at that. But perhaps something *could* be done about a memorial.

I tracked down the the Ox and Bucks Regimental Association. It was one of its committee members, Colonel Robin Evelegh, who had visited Aston abortively to look for Alfred's grave and through him I contacted the very active Regimental Secretary of the Association, Lieutenant Colonel Peter Chamberlin at his headquarters in Winchester. Peter felt that the Association would look kindly on a formal approach for help, so I set about putting together the bones of a proposition.

The Reverend Jolley proved to be a great help. Andy had given up his career as a successful management consultant to take Holy Orders and, eventually, to become Vicar of Aston Parish Church, in what must be confessed is a not particularly salubrious part of central Birmingham. But the torch he carries burns brightly amongst the kebab shops and old terraced houses of Aston and he set about helping with enthusiasm. He quickly told me that there would be no hope of putting a memorial up inside the church and a headstone could not be erected in the churchyard unless there was an appropriate grave beneath it. And, of course, we could not prove the grave site.

So no headstone – but a stone memorial of some kind? Yes, this was possible as long as we kept to the strict specifications laid down by the church, controlling the size (no more than four feet high, two feet wide and two inches deep) and type of stone. We gently sparred about the site and, after poring together over the venerable records of graves that did exist, agreed on an "empty" site, half way between where I believed Alf to lie and my father's own grave.

Andy and I agreed on the form of a simple ceremony for the dedication of the stone and I then set about creating a budget, to include a reception afterwards in a banqueting suite at the nearby Villa Park (I dismissed the heretical thought that Alf would have supported Birmingham City FC). The subsequent proposal was then put by me to a meeting of the committee of the Regimental Association in Oxford, presided over by its chairman General Sir Edward Jones, recently retired as Black Rod, which agreed to my suggestion that it should back the project to two thirds of its cost if I could persuade what was left of the family to provide the remaining third. The enthusiasm shown at that meeting by this group of distinguished and magnificent old soldiers was heart warming and I drove away from Oxford that day certain at last that Alf was going to be fittingly remembered.

One further problem remained. Some of my uncle's descendants still lived in the Midlands but others had scattered around the country. Many of my cousins and their spouses, indeed, I had not seen for more than fifty years and I was less than certain that a request for financial support for the memorial from a shadowy figure from the past would meet with enthusiasm. I need not have worried. Back came the cheques and letters of support and, indeed, the family's proportion of the cost was over subscribed.

There was one further twist in the tale, however. Chris Sutton, the local historian who had sparked off this exercise, had discovered via the internet that a Mr Vincent Nicholls, living in Kent, was claiming to be Alfred's illegitimate son and was anxious to make contact with Alf's surviving family. It seemed that the timing was coincidental and that he had no knowledge of the efforts being made to honour Alf's memory. This, indeed, was a bolt from the blue, for none of my cousins – even those who had lived with Alf in his final years – had heard of a "love child."

I have to confess that we were a touch suspicious. Looking back now, I am not quite sure why. There were no pecuniary rewards to be gained by claiming Alf as a parent, but the doubt remained that perhaps this was someone who was trying to claim a touch of reflected glory. After all, none of us – particularly my two cousins who had lived with our uncle – could recall a liaison that had produced a child.

Oh there were affairs, all right. Alfred remained a handsome man in middle age, of some celebrity, and for some time a glamorous woman in her late twenties had lived with him, whose long red finger nails sent at least this boy of twelve into lustful reveries. But a child? No!

We would have heard.

So it was that I arranged a meeting with Vincent and his two incredibly tall sons in London. At first glance I realised that he was the genuine article. Erect and smartly bearded, Vincent had the well remembered high cheekbones and eyes of my uncle. He showed me pictures of his mother, Alice Standford. She had been Alf's barmaid in one of the pubs and, hair tightly permed in contemporary style, with a tip-tilted *retroussé* nose, she would have tempted a saint. And, clearly, Alfred was no saint. It should be said, however, that he and Louise had parted years before and he was living alone. Alice clearly fell in love with him and wanted the child and Vincent was born in 1942.

Alf supported Alice and his son financially until she married four years later when Vincent adopted the name of his step father. Alice often talked to her son about his celebrated father but he had no direct memories of him, although Alfred regularly visited the two of them before Alice married.

Our meeting removed any doubts and Vincent and his family were warmly welcomed into what was left of the Wilcox clan and accepted the invitation to attend the dedication of his father's memorial in Aston churchyard on 12th September 2006.

The sun shone through the trees, still carrying late summer leaves, on that day as we all gathered round the white Portland stone memorial. It was, fittingly, exactly 88 years to the day since the action that had earned Alfred the cross. The inscription on the stone read: "For Valour. Near this site lies ALFRED WILCOX, 1884–1954, awarded the Victoria Cross for conspicuous bravery in France, 12th September 1918. This stone is erected in memory of an Aston born man by his family and his regiment, the Oxf & Bucks Lt Infty." The words were topped and tailed by engravings of the cross and the distinctive hunting horn badge of the regiment.

More than 50 people assembled around the stone. Twenty-six descendants of Alfred had come from as far away as Durham, Wiltshire, Nottingham, Harrogate, Maidstone, London, as well as the Midlands, and local dignitaries mingled with press reporters and camera crews. Equally, if not more importantly, a busload of the great and good of the regiment arrived from Oxford. They included two four star generals, one brigadier and a clutch of colonels and lieutenant colonels. Quite a turn-out for a lance-corporal!

It was a colourful as well as moving occasion. The bright dresses of the ladies contrasted with the severe black and white of the clergy, the green uniform of the Green Jackets bugler and the blue of the British Legion standard bearers. Vincent Nicholls, Alf's son, read the lesson and Elaine Read, his granddaughter, and General Sir Edward Jones together laid wreaths. Once again the Last Post echoed through the old churchyard as the Legion bearers dipped their standards and it seemed as though even the traffic of Spaghetti Junction had become muted for a minute in tribute.

Then we all adjourned to Villa Park to drink a toast to Alfred and his brothers. The generals and colonels mingled happily with the family and the local historians. As cousin Ray said, "Alf would have loved it."

It was closure for those of us who had sought to pin down Alf's last resting place. For me, however, that day in the churchyard, prompted something else. Remembering my awesome but jocular uncle, I heard again the moan of air raid sirens, the crack of anti-aircraft guns and tasted again dried egg, too-sweet tea and spam. The war years were there again and demanding to be recalled through the eyes of a young boy.

Chapter 2

"YOU DON'T HEAR THE ONE THAT GETS YOU"

I was playing in the garden with my great chum Baden Hickman on that sunny Sunday morning of 3rd September 1939. We had made little aeroplanes of plasticine and were simulating dog fights by the side of the newly built Anderson shelter. Something made me go inside, to find my mother and father staring at each other. They ignored me but Dad, yellow of complexion and now quite thin, slowly put his head in his hands and muttered, "I can't believe they would do it again." Once again we were at war with Germany.

It is difficult to imagine now what the announcement must have meant to those veterans of 1914–18. They had fought the Germans to a standstill in the mud of Flanders and France. They had seen their comrades and sometimes their brothers die. They had witnessed the tortuous cobbling together of a peace treaty and gone through a post war economic depression that had put millions out of work. Now, it would all have to be done again. But – *could* we do it again?

My father had no doubt.

His tuberculosis had been finally diagnosed in the early thirties, shortly after my birth, and in those days it was invariably a death sentence. The shrapnel that had exploded into his lungs as he trudged towards the wire in 1916 had never been removed (we learned later that a large piece had lodged near his liver and remained there). The consumption tightened its grip through the decade so that he was always coughing, his step seemingly getting slower by the month as he walked up the entry of our terraced house. He did, however, score one victory – pyrrhic but significant – over the disease.

I was playing under the table in our living room one day, hidden by the plush red chenille table cloth that fell to the floor, when I heard him come in and say to Mum:

"Well, Spike, we've done it." Some twenty years after sustaining his wounds, he had at last convinced a medical panel that his illness was due to the shellburst that had knocked him unconscious on that day in 1916. Mother would now receive a war widows' pension when he died – a sum considerably more than the ordinary widow's state pension. For my parents, struggling to bring up two children on the wage of a semi invalid, it was a back-handed, tragic kind of victory. Only by dying could my father provide a basic income for his family.

The disease was hugely debilitating, of course, and increasingly he had to spend longer periods in bed, coughing and spitting (sometimes blood) into the potty kept always near. He had long since lost his job as a skilled diamond mounter and his doctor had advised that, somehow, he must take work in the open air to help his breathing. The open air? What – work as a navvy, with *his* wasted frame?

Of course not, but the opportunities for outdoor work for a sick man were few. Eventually, father borrowed money and, for £100, bought an insurance "book," and began the doleful life of the door-to-door insurance collector.

Yet the fire that burned within my father never died. He had no physical energy, but the drive that had seeped from his body seemed to have been transferred to his brain. He had left school at thirteen with very little formal education but he now became an avid reader and self improver. I remember a huge tome arriving one day: "Dynamic Tension, the Secret of Life" – or something like that. The title was as incomprehensible to me then as it is today. But Dad absorbed it. He also developed an interest in – no, a passion for – politics. After years "going with his betters" and unthinkingly voting Conservative, he began to devour the newspapers and develop a hatred of the right wing politicians whom, he felt, had led us into the depression and failed to deliver a land "fit for heroes to live in" after the war. Not for him, though, a gradual drift away from the right. He swung compulsively and comprehensively to the left and went the whole hog. Although he never formally joined the party, Dad became a Communist and throughout most of the war we took the "Daily Worker," trimmed by Churchill to a little one fold, four pager. After Dad had finished with it every day I would devour it, as I did with Michael Foot's "Guilty Men," which in time inevitably found its way into our house.

Dad's politics may have changed but never his profound conviction that we would win the war. After that first moment of depression – "not again!" – that I witnessed, he followed every bend and twist of the land campaigns in, first, Europe, then North Africa and Russia and, finally, the Pacific and Europe again with never a doubt and mounting enthusiasm. His whoop of triumph when the wireless announced that Hitler had attacked Russia was memorable. "We've got the shitpot now," he bellowed up the stairs. (His language was completely unfettered and has always remained my excuse for my own shocking lapses. Although it should be said that Dad never used the f-word.)

In this study of the military campaigns of the war, I attempted to follow behind him, like Sancho on his donkey. The names of the cities, towns and villages that studded our advance, then our retreat, then our advance again along the Mediterranean coast line of North Africa remain imbedded in my memory: Sidi Barrani, Tobruk, Darnha, Marsa Susa, Benghazi, Bizerta and, of course, Alamein. He exhalted, of course, in the Battle of Britain and retained an unfailing confidence in the British Navy to see off the threat to our shipping posed by the U Boats in the Battle of the Atlantic. It was like living with a broken down nag who had once won the Grand National but who sniffed Aintree again every day.

The walking eventually became too much and he was forced to borrow again to buy a car so that he could continue to call on his customers and so carry on earning. Dad had no mechanical skills so it had to be a reliable vehicle, for there was no question of him being able to push the thing if it failed to start. It also had to be cheap, of course. The result was a black Ford 8, bought in about 1938 for £100 or thereabouts. The number plate was EOL 930, a monogram, his friends said, for "Easy Old Len rises at 9.30." For a time we delighted in weekend drives into the country with Dad, Toad-like, loving to extract as much speed as he could from his meagre eight horses and shouting at the "shitpots" in front who failed to change their gears as they struggled up hills, so slowing him down. In retrospect now, it is easy to forgive him his impatience. It was only behind the wheel, of course, that he could move quickly.

But the onset of war and the unavailability of petrol meant that the Ford had to be put away and Dad was back to walking his round again. His attacks of sickness, when his pepper-pot lungs refused to pump him around – and sometimes aggravated by complications such as stomach ulcers – became more frequent and mother increasingly had to add the role of insurance collector to those of housewife, mother and nurse. She did this with a composure and lack of obvious complaint that, looking back now, seems saint-like.

Florence ("Spike" came from my father and referred to her small but rather sharp nose) Pemberton was born in 1895, two years after her husband. She was a small, dark woman, with large beautiful eyes that lit up at the prospect of a family party but which usually gave her a melancholy air. It could be said, indeed, that she had had plenty to be melancholy about. Her father had died at the age of 31 (of consumption, of course) and from the age of about eleven, as the oldest child, she worked with her mother, who earned a kind of living to pay for the upkeep of herself and her four children by taking in washing and scrubbing steps. Florence went to school only when she could, which did not stop her from developing the most cultured handwriting and a love of reading, although she rarely ventured beyond Ethel M. Dell. Her late teens and early twenties, a time for most girls of gaiety and falling in love, coincided with the Great War and, as the casualty lists grew, there were no more family parties. Her young brother, Will, was killed at the age of 19 as a stretcher-bearer at the Battle of the Somme. Her other brother, Leonard, was blessedly too young to fight but the Reaper didn't let him escape. He was killed in a motor accident in 1934. Her young sister Ada was a different kind of casualty from the war. She never married. There was, she used to say, "just nobody left..."

So mother was used to, if not prepared for, adversity when she met my father. The illness, of course, had not developed then and, in fact, he was never invalided out of the army, returning from the front to end the war as a drill instructor. They were undoubtedly a gregarious and happy couple, Mother's sad family compensated for by the welcoming and large Wilcox clan, whose penchant for parties, singing and dancing soon brought a sparkle to those pensive large eyes. These were the days before radio and television, of course, and home entertainment was very much self-created. Everyone had his own song and Leonard, who could play the piano well by ear, would accompany as Spike sang "Just a Song at Twilight." They married and, in 1923, Margaret Mary was born. Later, they were able to move out of Aston when they secured the tenancy of a new council house in Kingstanding and then, in 1931, I was born – a "mistake," I was to learn, because there was little money, but, it seems, a happy one. Then came the depression, father's job loss and, of course, the dreaded sentence of tuberculosis.

And yet, my sister and I could not have wished for a more loving home in which to grow up. The reason seems to have been that, undemonstrative as they were, Leonard and Florence loved each other with an undeviating devotion that survived all their adversity. In fact, it is a touch misleading to say that they were undemonstrative. It was true of mother, who was deeply loving of us but who, one sensed, was always rather embarrassed by a show of emotion. Not so father. He would kiss us all roundly on the lips at bedtime and "liked a cuddle."

There was another element that, despite the ever-present threat of Dad's illness, usually made our home a happy environment. This was my father's sense of humour. He was a genuinely funny man who enlivened any party. He had an unusually large head so that most hats to be found in any household would perch on his crown like a pea on a potato and would provide the prop for a series of witticisms delivered with the straightest of faces. Given an audience and (later, when he had given up abstinence) a pint of mild, he would forget his illness and convulse any audience. It could be said, I guess, that on one of his shoulders sat the spectre with the hood and the scythe; on the other, the clown with the cap and bells. He was a very funny, life-loving man who breathed – or, in later life, wheezed – emotion and love.

Mother's mother in her sixties was having difficulty in making ends meet and so we moved from the smart little council house to live with her in her grim, mid-Victorian terraced house in Tower Road, Aston. Then, when this proved unbearable (three pokey bedrooms for six people and, of course, no bathroom) we moved on, half a mile away, to rent a house of our own in Ettington Road, still in Aston.

The street and the house still stands, somehow having been spared the high rise development that was to have been the post-war architectural saviour of inner city districts like Aston. Built perhaps at the end of the nineteenth century, the street consisted of two rows of brick terraces, each house identical to the next. A tiny strip of front garden, usually guarded by a privet hedge, was matched at the back by a rather larger rectangle of lawn. Still no bathroom or running hot water, of course, but there was a scullery and the inevitable outdoor loo. If it wasn't for the number above the door and the selection of front room curtain, you would be hard put to know from the street which house was yours. But not today. Structurally, the houses haven't changed but now individualism reigns. Each house seems to be painted a different colour and, in addition, the front doors sing an additional hymn to the paint brush. The Asians who live there now seem to be trying each to outdo the other in creativity and *joie de vivre*. When I visited in 2007, I liked it all. Better, I felt, than in 1938.

On that visit, my wife and I paused outside our old house, painted now a strange but not unpleasant mustard yellow. We decided not to knock on the door because we felt that that would be an intrusion. But as an old lady and what was obviously her youngish middle-aged daughter, dressed in saris, walked up the pavement towards us, I felt a little guilty to be gawping so I explained, "I lived in this house more than sixty years ago." I was not understood, so, a little abashed, I repeated my reason for standing and staring on what was obviously their street. In fact, it was not just their street for my old house was now *their* house. The old lady frowned, revealed three teeth and muttered, "this *my* home." Then she walked by without further eye contact. Betty and I exchanged glances and walked away. Ettington Road was now part of another world and, of course, sentimental nostalgia gave us no claim on it now.

We were living at number 64 Ettington Road when war was declared. In those anxious days, the word was that the bomber would always get through. As the British Expeditionary Force was hastily assembled and despatched to France, nearby Aston Park became a home for searchlight batteries and anti-aircraft emplacements and fat, silver barrage balloons appeared, bobbing about 400 feet above our roof tops. A precocious student of warfare defences, I could never see the point of these strange dirigibles and I used to lecture Baden on their uselessness. Bombs wouldn't bounce off them and they were tethered too low to deter altitude bombers. And dive bombers would surely pull out of their dives above the balloons before they released their bombs? So… what were they for? Baden didn't know and neither did I. The stupid things disappeared about six months later so perhaps I had a point.

What was incontrovertible, however, was that we were now in the front line. Birmingham was an industrial city, the second largest in the country, and was home to a thousand and one small manufacturing trades. More than that, however, it also housed large factories which had hurriedly switched to making weapons, tanks and aircraft: Hercules, Austin, Kynoch, Dunlop et al. And Aston, close to the inner city in the north east corner, was slap in the middle of these industrial giants. Aston was a target area and we were living more or less in the bulls eye.

Hurried plans were made to evacuate the children of the city to the country, away from the bombs, and my school in Albert Road closed to become an administrative centre for the great move. My sister Margaret, of course, had left school years before and was working as a filing clerk at the General Electric Company but I was eligible to join the exodus. My mother was having none of it. The family, she said, was not to be broken up under any circumstances. If Hitler's bombs were going to kill some of us then they would kill all of us, but her eight year old was not leaving home, thank you very much. So I stayed and, to my joy, my friend Baden who now lived next door, stayed behind, too. This period of "the phoney war," when the armies of France and Britain and Germany stood inactively facing each other across the Maginot Line, became a kind of paradise for the two of us. There was no school, no bombing (yet) and we were allowed to play all day in the nearby park and the streets around home.

This Eden ended as 1940 dawned and school of a kind was established for about eight of us in a little house in neighbouring Whitehead Road, home of one of the boys from the school who had also not been evacuated. There, gathered around a table in Mrs Johnson's parlour, we sat under the eye of tall, gaunt Mr Clifford, one of the older teachers at the school. It was he who, before the outbreak of war, had given permission for one of the girls in class to leave early so that she could say good-bye to her father, who was joining his regiment. "It is right she should go," he confided to the class after she had left, "because she may never see her father again." I remember thinking then that the old man had gone a bit too far – after all, the war hadn't even started! But looking back now, I guess that Clifford must have been a veteran of the First World War and dreaded a repeat of the slaughter. In that little front parlour, anyway, he was very close to us all. Every day I could see the little blue veins on his nose. There were no chewing of sweets and whispered jokes as in school classes. We had to buckle down. The holiday was over.

So, too, shortly afterwards, was the Phoney War. Hitler swept through the Low Countries and then France as Dad's call for "some bloody action" was answered, but not in the way he wished. The war had become real, at last, as the pathetic remnants of the BEF were ferried home in bits and pieces from Dunkirk. The Germans were massing to invade across the Channel and my nine-year-old sensibility was well aware of this. But I was certainly not afraid. I could not bring myself to hate the enemy. The newspapers and my comics were full of the atrocities perpetrated by the Gestapo who had even parachuted down into Holland dressed as nuns! Somehow, I could not believe all of this. The Germans were ordinary people, just like us, weren't they? And ordinary people could talk to each other and, somehow, get on, couldn't they?

We, like many families with gardens, had been issued with the materials for an Anderson shelter just before the outbreak of hostilities. These consisted of six corrugated steel sheets, bent over at the end so that they could be bolted together to form, with separate endpieces, a vaulted shelter. With the steels came instructions. A shallow pit, some three feet deep by ten feet long by four and half feet wide, was to be dug, and the corrugated sheets bolted together within it. Earth then was to be heaped onto the sheets to a depth of about fifteen inches on the top and thirty inches on the side. The resulting shelter, half in and half projecting out of the ground, measured about six feet (1.8 metres) high, four and a half feet (1.4 metres) wide and six and a half feet (2 metres) long. It provided cramped accommodation for six people and was said to provide safe shelter for anything but a direct hit.

By September 1940 more than 2.3 million had been distributed to something like 27% of the population – including the Wilcoxes of 64 Ettington Road. Those with an annual income of less than £250 received their shelters free. Those above that stipend paid a token £7.

I have no idea whether we paid or not. The problem for us lay in erecting it, because Dad could not lift a spade to save his life – as seemed the precise requirement.

That difficulty, however, was solved by the decision of our neighbours to pool all their steel sheet resources to form one large, communal shelter in the garden of No 68, the home of Mrs Mack, an elderly and delightful Scottish lady who lived alone, except for her lodger, a young woman whose husband had escaped from Dunkirk.

The men, with the exception of my father, set to erect this long, low shelter, big enough to house some twenty people. I never did know whether this was done specifically to help the Wilcoxes. I fancy that this may have been the catalyst, but certainly other families without fit, young men at the helm, benefited and I remember the buzz of conviviality that surrounded the whole enterprise. Gaps were cut in our garden fences so that we could all have easy access and cane chairs and benches were installed, as well as paraffin heaters. If bombing did start, then at least we would all have company in the night hours and a mutual support system if the worst happened.

The long, low bunker sat unused all through the summer of 1940 and to Baden and me it was merely a large grassy lump in Mrs Mac's garden, serving us as the Sheriff of Nottingham's castle or the site of Custer's Last Stand. Another addition to the landscape was a large (about 30ft in length, 10ft wide and some 5ft deep) steel, open-topped tank that suddenly appeared in the road outside our house. Filled with water, it provided a ready supply for the Fire Brigade should incendiary bombs take hold. It also provided a useful backdrop on which to chalk cricket stumps and kick a ball as we played through that long summer of 1940. Then the autumn closed in. That was when the war closed in, too, for the people of Ettington Road.

The first heavy air raids on Birmingham began in October and set a pattern that was to be repeated through until February 1941. The wailing moan of the alarm sirens (the "all clear" was a continuous, flat sound) began at about 7.30pm, conveniently after the families had had their high tea, and we would all make our way, carrying blankets and thermos flasks, to "Mrs Mac's hump." At first, it was fun. Baden and I would bring books and puzzles and the smell of paraffin and general dampness would trigger a sense of adventure. Being allowed to stay up, on its own, was an indulgence and it was good to sit and listen to the grown-up talk. Then, as the ritual was repeated night after night, the hardness of the benches, the dampness, the cold and the poor light from the oil lamps, closed in on us all, so that eventually our semi-underground cavern became a place of misery and anxiety.

The discomfort was particularly acute for my father. He had little flesh to cover his bones, anyway, and he struggled to sit upright through the night, despite the cushions that were piled all around him. His coughing, of course, was frequent and must have been a constant irritant, at the least, to those around him. The idea of having a communal shelter now no longer seemed such a good idea. We knew that the families who had erected their own, four or six person shelter, had been able to furnish them with bunks of a sort – the thought of which offered comfort beyond belief to those of us forced to sit and loll upright for hours on end. In the end, Dad refused to leave his bed and said that he would rather be blown to bits in comparative comfort than retreat to "that bloody torture chamber." But that was later. First, we had the bombs.

The German aircraft came in waves. We could hear them quite distinctly and they were immediately recognisable because their diesel engines gave out a rhythmical, throbbing sound – *woa-woa-woa-woa* – markedly different from the continuous whine of the British planes. Not that there were any of those about during those early winter nights. This was before the airborne radar sets had been perfected for our night fighters, so, initially, it was just the searchlights and the ack ack guns against the Heinkels and Dorniers – and the attackers always won, or so it seemed to us. Throughout the night bombing of Birmingham, I don't remember any of the intruders being hit by anti-aircraft fire, although it gave comfort of a sort to hear the guns firing. Perhaps they were some sort of deterrent, anyway, forcing the bombers to remain high.

The Germans had fitted scream devices to the fins of the bombs so that one could hear the bloody things hurtling down, growing louder as they neared their targets. The idea, of course, was to create terror amongst the civilian population, crouching in their shelters – and, by golly, we did crouch as we heard those screams in the night. It was almost impossible to avoid hunching the shoulders instinctively and bending the head as the noise grew louder.

"Don't worry, you don't hear the one that gets you!" This was Mr Jewkes. I disliked Mr Jewkes. He was an elderly, small, bald headed man with a silvery moustache cut in the manner of Ronald Colman. He knew everything and shared most of it with his captive audience in the shelter. I can't remember whether there was a Mrs Jewkes. If there were, she must have had a hell of a time because he never stopped pontificating to the rest of us. I disliked the man, not only for his know-it-all behaviour, but because he always chewed the end of his cigarette. I found that disgusting, though I learned to keep quiet about him because Dad was quick to stamp out any criticism I might make of the grown-ups. He hated precocious behaviour.

We had no toilet in the shelter, of course, and during one particularly heavy raid Mr Jewkes had waited for a lull in the attacks before creeping out into the alien night to use the facilities in his house. His expedition coincided with a particularly heavy attack and, as the screaming bombs seemed to fall all around us, I confess that I giggled with glee at the thought of Mr J. sitting on his throne, defenceless and very, very vulnerable.

But, wouldn't you know it, in the inevitable lull that followed, the little man bounced back, pulling aside the blanket that covered the entrance, his bald head wearing a light coating of plaster and his cigarette chewed, it seemed, almost to nothing. He stood for a moment in the entrance, rocking slightly on his heels. Then he jabbed his finger along the lines of silent faces regarding him.

"Your house is down," he said, "and yours, and yours. Most of the street's gone. They've got us this time."

It was rubbish. Bombs had fallen nearby, it is true, but Ettington Road had escaped again, although, despite the brown sticky paper with which we had criss-crossed our windows, many panes had been blown out by the bomb blasts. Mr Jewkes's reputation as a source of information and knowledge had already worn thin but that night saw it disappear for ever.

Apart from a quick dash to the lavatory, I was not allowed out during the raids, of course. But the night of 14th November was comparatively quiet for us. An early wave or two had come over but nothing after midnight and my father called me to come outside to join him at the mouth of the shelter. "Look at this, son," he said, pointing to the south east. It was indeed, an unforgettable sight. It seemed as though the horizon was on fire, the white and the red of the glare stretching for what looked like many miles. As I watched, flashes of fire sprang up to illuminate the base of the clouds and we could hear a constant dull thumping, as though a battery of hydraulic drills were operating half a mile or so away.

"It must be Coventry, Len," said Mr Hickman. And so it proved. It was the night that the word "Coventration" was coined.

For ten hours, from 7.30pm, 500 German bombers in successive waves targeted the city and dropped 30,000 incendiaries, 500 tons of high explosives, 50 landmines and 20 oil mines on it. Two hundred individual fires in the city centre converged into one and blazed through the night, destroying the centuries old cathedral amongst many other fine buildings. In all, 554 people – mainly civilians – lay dead and 865 were injured. The Germans code-named the attack, "Operation Moonlight." Perhaps they were thinking of the Sonata?

These statistics seem insignificant today compared to the Allied bombing of Dresden much later in the war, and, of course, the carnage caused by the bombs dropped on Hiroshima and Nagasaki, or even to the intensity of the German attacks through 1940–41 on London. But this individual raid on Coventry was Britain's first experience of total war, the German blitzkrieg pioneered on Guernica during the Spanish civil war. The precisely focussed barbarity of it, with its indiscriminate killing of civilians, shocked everyone and presaged what was to come.

It seemed that everyone in Birmingham knew someone who had either been killed, injured or who had survived the Coventry raid. The two cities, after all, were only some eighteen miles apart, just an inch on my school atlas. My second cousin, Albert, had a sister whose boyfriend lived in Coventry. He came through the bombing all right but his happy little Scots terrier did not. Scotty was the most friendly of tail-wagging little dogs. He spent 14th November in a shelter as the bombs screamed down all around – and he emerged a snappy, vicious, psychopath of a mongrel who eventually had to be put down. A tiny casualty only, but symptomatic of the fall out from that dreadful night.

It seemed as though Coventry somehow had unlocked the doors of hell for us in Birmingham – or maybe showed the Germans exactly where we were, for the intensity of the raids on our city seemed to increase after that night. Before the Coventry attack, we occasionally had a blessed night when the sirens did not sound and we were able to sleep through the night in our beds. This happened perhaps once in every ten nights. But not after Coventry. Every night afterwards, without remission until Christmas, my memory tells me that we huddled together in our damp shelter, jokeless now and glumly aware of what was to come.

One particular night – I cannot recall the date but it was as Christmas neared, as though to remind us that Christianity had nothing to do with what was happening – was worse even than the night Mr Jewkes lost his reputation for veracity. Wave after wave of the bombers droned overhead and the screaming bombs seemed to be creeping ever nearer to us. Even our sturdy shelter now began to shake as explosions occurred all around. One particular bomb seemed to begin its fall louder than the others and I believe everyone eschewed Jewkes and felt "this is the one." Mother threw me to the floor of the shelter and hurled herself on top of me. She remained small (about 5ft 2ins) but she had put on weight in middle age and I remember thinking, as my cheek was pressed to the rough hessian matting, that I would rather be killed by a German bomb than be suffocated by my mother. The device exploded with a huge crump, shaking us all and blowing out the paraffin lamps. I lay there in the dark as everyone was screaming and I began singing "Roll Out the Barrel" in an attempt to… do what? I don't know. Perhaps to impress my father, who never showed any sign of fear at any time. It had the desired effect, for I felt him pat my head and heard him say "Good lad."

In fact, it has to be said that I never felt afraid, throughout all the bombing. Again, I don't know why, because I was a very imaginative child and could easily imagine being buried alive under tons of rubble as often as I thrilled with horror at being forced by pirate's cutlass to walk the plank over a shark infested sea. Maybe it was the thought that those nice, ordinary Germans would never really want to kill me, of all people.

My school kept open throughout the blitz, dammit, and we were always expected to turn up promptly at nine a.m. every weekday morning, complete with gas masks, whatever the ravages of the night. But mother took pity on me on many mornings and let me sleep on, to the detriment, I have always firmly believed (until recently), of my grasp of arithmetic and mathematics. It was the tiredness and the all-pervading dampness of nights spent virtually underground that I remember most, looking back now. Sleeping in a chair was somehow never possible for me, except perhaps for the occasional ten minutes. Even now, I cannot sleep in aeroplanes – not even when, on rare indulgences, I have flown first class. And I acquired in those long, leg-numbing nights, a vulnerability to rheumatism that pounds in on me now, in old age.

But we were much luckier than others. Ettington Road survived the bombing, although houses were flattened in adjacent roads. Baden and I (when I managed to wake up, that is) rejoiced in roaming the streets picking up the jagged pieces of shrapnel that gave evidence of the activity of the anti-aircraft guns in the nearby park. With the imperturbable optimism of youth we never feared that one day a bomb would get us.

One evening, Dad bundled us into his Ford (somehow, in these early days of the war, he was still able to keep it on the road), and we drove off into Warwickshire until he found a bed and breakfast establishment which was able to take us. That night, at least, we had undisturbed sleep but he could not afford to do that every night, of course, and it was back to the hard cushions and cane chairs the next day. We spent two nights at Christmas 1940 at my grandmother's house, gambling that there would be a seasonable hiatus in the attacks, for grannie had no Anderson and her refuge during the bombing was her dank coal cellar. The gamble paid off, but 1941 stretched ahead of us and I remember sitting by that black leaded fire grate, back at 3 Tower Road, colouring in my Wizard of Oz book and wondering "how long can it all go on?"

Dad, at least, decided that he was not going to wait for the answer to that question. By January, we had moved again, to a clone of grandmother's house, equally old and grim-looking, in nearby Potters Hill, where I was destined to stay for the next twelve years. In retrospect, I think we moved because it was cheaper than Ettington Road (I used to take round twelve shillings and sixpence (now 63 pence) every week to the Potters Hill landlord, Mr Southall), for money must have been very tight. But – delight upon delight! – in our new, small garden was a conventional, family size Anderson shelter, complete with four cord-strung bunks!

In fact, we spent little time there. By now, Dad was fatalistic about death – he knew that it wasn't too far away for him, anyway – and he decided that he would stay in his bed through the raids, although he insisted that mother, Margaret and I should take shelter. But the attacks now began to dwindle until, by the end of January 1941 they were the exception rather than the rule and by February they had ceased altogether. I now had to find another excuse for being late for school.

All things are relative and I guess that Birmingham was luckier in the war than one or two other large cities, certainly Coventry and London, in that we were never left with such huge swathes of bomb damaged sites as they were. Certainly we were never rendered homeless like the East Enders we saw on the Pathe newsreel at the Odeon, although, as my mother used to say, "we had our share."

But the bombing – the very *personal* nature of it, with my wretched father being ushered shivering down the stairs into that damp shelter every night and my own legs aching with incipient rheumatism – changed my view of the Germans. Oh, I was quite prepared to believe still that, underneath everything, the ordinary German people were just like us, really, amiable folk with whom, despite language differences, we were bound to have much in common. But it was quite clear that these ordinary folk were letting their leaders unleash the most terrible kind of warfare. Even to my unformed mind, indiscriminate, mass bombing was clearly an abomination. Would gas attacks come next?

Side by side with my indignation, even perhaps stemming from it, grew a conviction that now we would certainly win the war. I had always been a touch cynical of Dad's enthusiastic support of Churchill. The Prime Minister was a Tory, wasn't he, and wasn't it the Tories who had brought on the depression and left us completely unprepared to fight Hitler? But we had now thrown off the threat of invasion and survived the bombing. True, things looked awful abroad with Japan now in the war and threatening Singapore and with our forces in North Africa in full retreat. Yet we would win through in the end. After all, we *were* British, weren't we? And those big battleships, *the Nelson* and *the Rodney,* had three of their main 16 inch gun turrets in their bows and only one in the stern, because, as everyone knew, the British Navy never retreated, only advanced. *Of course we would win!*

Chapter 3

YES, WE HAVE NO BANANAS…

W̶e had survived the bombing somehow but, to this now rather plump ten-year-old, a new threat – no, a direct blight, more painful than the Blitz – began to bite. Food rationing had been introduced on 8th January 1940 and each family's little buff coloured ration books had become far more important items of documentation than passports or birth certificates. By January of 1941 they were as precious as gold and, indeed, items of currency on the Black Market.

At first, the bite was not too deep, although painful enough. Each person was allowed four ounces of butter or lard per week, twelve ounces of sugar, four ounces of bacon or ham and two eggs. Shortly afterwards, however, meat was included (one shilling and ten penceworth (9p today) per person per week) and later rationing was extended to include tea, jam and marmalades, cheese and milk. In June 1941, sugar was cut further to eight ounces, eggs to one a week and meat reduced finally to one shilling's worth per week. Then the government announced that no more fruit would be imported – no bananas, pineapples, lemons or grapes and a few oranges for young children only. Only home grown fruit in season, such as apples, pears and cherries, could be provided by Mr Henney, our Scottish greengrocery man in Potters Hill.

For me, this was (literally) hitting below the belt. How could this egg-loving, sweet-toothed tub of a boy be expected to live on one egg per week and just one spoonful of sugar in his tea? It was preposterous! Naturally my mother shared this balanced view and immediately swung into action to ensure that her spoilt youngest's sufferings were not too great. As a result, the other members of the family sacrificed their sugar ration so that I was able to continue to put four heaped spoons full in my tea and someone always gave up an egg so that I could have at least two per week. I shudder now at my selfishness.

Householders had to register for food with their local shops. The shopkeeper was then, in theory, provided with enough food for his or her registered customers.

It was a complicated system which, certainly in the early days, led to abuse. Eggs used for breeding purposes and therefore exempt from rationing often found their way onto the market and ration books were not difficult to forge. Some unscrupulous postmen were not above stealing ration coupons and then selling them on. The phrase "Black Market" was on everyone's lips. So too was "under the counter." Specially favoured customers would be quietly slipped a little something – a few more eggs, perhaps or an extra cut of meat – into their bags by the shopkeeper. This would always be carefully wrapped in newspaper under the counter and, although it was always paid for, the housewife would have no idea what treat was enclosed until she arrived back home.

As the war continued, so the list of rationed foods grew. Items such as rice, canned fruit, condensed milk, breakfast cereals and biscuits were added to the list and jam and other preserves were rationed as a group, so that customers could choose to buy either jam, marmalade or syrup. Even soap was eventually rationed. We were all allowed one small tablet per month.

Bathing came under the stern eye of Whitehall, too. An edict was issued that hot water should be limited to five inches per bathtub per person. I remember asking to myself "who would know, outside the family?" It was widely publicised that the royal family in Buckingham Palace adhered strictly to this rule, the point being, presumably, that this was an example we should all follow. It was very academic in our case, anyway. We had no bathroom or running hot water, of course, and taking a bath meant bringing down from the outside lavatory the large tin bath that hung there, depositing it before the coal fire in the parlour and filling it with steaming saucepans that mother (mother, of course, did *everything*) brought from the coal fired copper in the kitchen. We were lucky to get three inches to splash in, let alone five!

Eventually coupons became necessary for the purchase of clothes and the scarcity of textiles imposed new disciplines. Young couples engaged to be married now not only saved their pennies but their coupons for the wedding dress too. New fashions sprang from the shortages. Patches were sewn onto knitwear jumpers and tweed sports jackets and suits to enable them to be worn longer – an economy which remains to this day as part of the country look.

Women suffered particularly from the absence of silk for stockings (nylons, at this time of resolute cracking down on non-essentials, stayed firmly in the land of their birth, the USA). All kinds of bucolic subterfuges were attempted by girls and women desperate to resist the fading of this last touch of glamour from their lives. I remember cycling out to the edge of Birmingham to fill two small sacks with fine sand from a building site to bring back to my sister Margaret. We mixed the sand with water and applied it to her shaven legs. Then she used eyebrow pencil to simulate the seam down the back of her legs. It was all washed off at night but it must have been grittily uncomfortable. She bore it for a few days… until the rains came.

There *were* relaxations in the rationing code, however. Milk was in short supply, due in part to the slaughter of dairy herds during 1940 to allow more land to be used for arable farming, but, even so, the government introduced a scheme early in 1941 to give free milk to children in schools, equal to one third of a pint for each child. In my school we called it the lunch break (dinner, of course, was taken at mid-day and the evening meal was "tea") and mother would give me a small jam sandwich to eat with the milk. I salivate now at the memory of the scrumptious contrast of the sweetness of the black currant jam against the cold, creamy milk.

A by-product of the petrol shortage – coupons were only allowed now for people who used their cars on essential business for the war effort – was the return to the streets of horses to pull the milk floats. This was welcome to Baden and me for we began a profitable business of cleaning up the horse manure and selling it to gardeners who were "digging for victory." We charged a penny a bag, enough to buy liquorice whirls or mixed peppermints from Mr Harris's shop at the top of Potter's Hill – if, that is, Mr Harris had managed to replenish his stocks and if we had sufficient sweet coupons in our ration books. For sweets had become rationed too; a further example of Hitler's personal vindictiveness towards me.

Oh, how I yearned for the chocolate bars that were now a thing of the past! Choc ices became a particular mystical Holy Grail, elevated in my memory to the delicious unattainable, a reward that might possibly be returned to me one day if I was good – and, of course, if we won the war, whenever that would be. As the war went on, I met young boys who did not remember bananas and to whom I had to explain what a choc ice meant. I took this responsibility seriously, for it was important to maintain the memory of these essentials. How ridiculous, I would reflect, for boring bread not to be rationed (this happened, amazingly, after the war, as late as 1946, and did not come off the ration list until 1948) while choc ices had been banned so early by the food controllers. The War Cabinet clearly had serious problems with its priorities.

I was not alone in my attempt to keep the flame alight. Those luxuries that were once part of our daily lives and taken for granted now became enshrined in popular culture. The banana, in particular, was immortalised in song. Hardly a day passed, it seemed, without the radio blaring out:

(To be sung with a jolly, fast paced lilt)
"Yes, we have no bananas,
We have no bananas, today."
Or:
(To be rendered softly, as a lament)
"Oh when can I have a banana again?
Tell me mother, do.
When can I have a banana again?

Like we used to do.
I like them for breakfast, I like them for lunch,
I like them single or all in a bunch.
Oh when can I have a banana again?
Tell me mother, do."

Mother couldn't tell me and neither could anyone else, although Dad tried to explain that, although the Japanese had taken Malaya and were swarming up Burma, the fact that America *and* Russia were now in the war meant that we, together with China, Japan's long standing enemy, now outnumbered the Axis powers and it was inevitable that we would win the war. Well, I knew that, stupid, but how long, dear God, how long before I could have a choc ice again?

The government now set about attempting to fill the holes left in the nation's diet with new, manufactured dishes. Nothing as sensible, of course, as a substitute for Aero bars and choc ices, but strange new products like "dried milk powder", which was mixed with water as a substitute for real milk, and, from America (where else?), dried egg powder. For one shilling and nine pence, one could buy a packet equivalent to twelve eggs. Actually, I grew to love this and was wolfing it down as late as 1951 when I left home to do my National Service in the army. Later in the war, whale meat crept onto the butchers' counters (or was it the slate of the wet fish shop?), even horse meat too made an appearance, as did the much more respectable canned, compacted meat product called spam, mainly consisting of ham and since immortalised by Monty Python.

Life was hell for housewives and mothers, because having coupons in their ration books did not in any way guarantee that food would be available at the shop to which they were registered. As supplies ran out, so shops would close and only open, say, for three or four days a week. This meant that queues would form outside shops early in the morning on the rumour that they had had a delivery of a certain commodity. For my mother, acting as locum for my father when he was ill and for all mothers who had jobs, this kind of lottery imposed physical and emotional burdens that today would have demanded counselling. But mother, like the rest, just "got on with it." What else was there to do? There was a war on, wasn't there?

In fact, mother displayed an ingenuity in menu planning that would have graced a British Army quartermaster in the retreat from Coruna. Tea was re-used as many times as possible and a "pennorth of scratchings" (well roasted pig's skin) sometimes became the meat to accompany the two veg. Offal was not rationed and neither was indigenous game. Lamb's brains, then, incongruously appeared on our table at tea time and rabbit in various guises became the staple of our weekly dinner fare, with "a bit of fish" – also not rationed – on Fridays. In fact, looking back now to the war years, the dishes I remember most often are dried eggs on toast, and rabbit followed by rhubarb and custard.

My parents had never eaten out, except in their courting days when they would snatch something on toast at a café in town before going to see the latest Chaplin or Keaton. They were therefore completely unaffected by the imposition of a ceiling price of five shillings per meal placed on restaurants, which were only allowed to serve one course. Later in the war, these refuges of the better off were supplemented by enterprises administered by local authorities called British Restaurants. These strange hybrids were often set up in schools and church halls and they were run on a non-profit making basis. As a result, they completely lacked any service frills and eschewed any attempt at creating ambience.

They also stayed firmly within the Food Ministry's rules in that only one course could be served of either meat, poultry, fish, eggs or cheese. I visited one such establishment just once, towards the end of the war. I remember that it was like eating in a long, low shed and there I had my first meeting with Heinz canned beans. I thought they were horrible. Now I doubt if I could live without them.

So how did all this austerity and belt tightening leave us? Did we become a nation of underfed weaklings, losing pounds and will-power as a result of substituting egg powder *et al* for the real thing?

Well, it is true that I had lost all my puppy fat by the time I was fourteen in the last year of the war. But this would have happened anyway with the onset of adolescence. In fact, statistics and medical records showed that the nation was much healthier as it emerged from the war. In the depression-ridden thirties, the poorer people of the urban population were not able to feed themselves properly but the better wages of wartime, plus the absence of the men, away eating heartily in the services, enabled the rest of the civilian population to live comparatively well. Equally important, the wartime diet amazingly proved to be good for us all. People ate less fat and more vegetables. The average calorie intake fell from 3,000 to 2,800 a day. As the rationing system settled down and became more targeted, special food, drink and vitamin supplements were introduced for pregnant women and babies and infant mortality fell from 51 to 46 per thousand live births during the war. John Bull had become leaner, more healthy.

Mind you, I would have given a year of my healthy adolescence for just one choc ice.

Chapter 4

"THE BEST GOVERNED CITY IN THE WORLD"

My mother's father died of tuberculosis, as I have recorded, at the age of 31. This was contracted, my mother told me, from contamination of the lungs caused by the steel filings he inhaled in his place of work, *his bedroom,* where he sanded down rifle barrels for about ten hours a day.

The story was related to me with a touch of pride. There was no sad admission that this was a terrible way to earn a living or, indeed, that it reflected an inappropriate, if necessary, intrusion into the sanctity of home life. No, to mother, my grandfather was an independent, free-lance artisan, his own master to a large extent, who was making his way in the world until this awful, so prevalent disease of the time struck him down. Just bad luck, really. And it was bad luck that he had not been able to put enough money aside before he died to prevent his wife and twelve-year-old daughter from having to scrub steps to earn a living.

William Pemberton, then, was very much a man of his time – and a man of Birmingham. Manchester had grown on the back of cotton, Bradford owed its prosperity to wool, Glasgow to ship building, Leeds to tailoring, Sheffield to steel and Leicester to knitwear. But Birmingham owed allegiance to no single industry. By 1849, more than 500 classes of manufacture and some 2,000 hardware trades gave what a Board of Health Commissioner at the time called 'exceptional elasticity to the trade of the town.' Work was carried on in hundreds of small workshops (even, it seems, in bedrooms) rather than great factories.

One result was that relations between masters and men were close, if not always harmonious. John Collins, a local Chartist remarked that Birmingham was a place where 'large manufacturers cannot shut up their men as they can in Manchester.' One London journalist recorded in the 1850s that 'small household trades existed which gave the inmates independence and often led – if trade continued to be good – to competence or fortune.'

Alas, Will Pemberton didn't have the health or the time to surge on towards competence or fortune. He did, however, reflect the independence of the people who worked in the city, an independence that went hand-in-hand with strong non-conformism in religion and radicalism in politics. Both were to fashion a city that sprang ahead in the second half of the nineteenth century in a way that astonished the rest of the country and created a new concept of civic ambition.

The philosophy was given the tag of 'the civic gospel,' a title that reflected, of course, the huge importance of religion in Victorian Britain. At a time when the national exchequer gave little financial help to local government, a new type of town councillor picked up the reins in Birmingham and determined to shape the city himself, even if it meant taking risks that had never before been contemplated in the council chamber. Local businessmen and entrepreneurs with successful records in commerce now stood for election and removed the plodding shopkeepers and tradesmen who before had dominated local politics and whose ambitions were limited to parochial issues.

Local politics in Birmingham, such as it was, had always been radical and loosely housed within the Liberal Party. Now, however, a strong discipline was instilled in the Party which took the form of a caucus that dominated local party associations and the Town Council itself, subjugating most issues to a clearly defined overall policy. At this time, the policy was municipal expansion. The Council had become a forum for doers, rather than talkers and, within the space of fifteen years, the life of the city changed beyond all recognition.

One man led the way and personified the new approach. Joseph Chamberlain had come to Birmingham in 1854 at the age of eighteen and quickly established a reputation as a successful businessman. He emerged into public life by being active in the field of education and was elected to the Town Council in 1869 and became Mayor four years later. 'Joe,' as he became known to millions throughout the world as his career progressed, looked the part of a leader. Tall, impeccably dressed – he once appeared at a public meeting wearing a sealskin topcoat – monocle screwed into one eye and invariably sporting an orchid in his buttonhole, Chamberlain was no great orator. But he was 'a doer.' His surging energy, his intellect, his single mindedness and, above all, his confidence in himself and his policies carried all before him in the previously passive world of civic politics.

His achievements were prodigious. He helped to create a big Central Reference Library in 1866 and then, under his leadership, the Council bought out in 1874 the two gas companies supplying the city and took over that function, paying for the purchase from future profits; implemented a sorely needed sewage disposal system in 1875; municipalized the water supply in 1876 and began a land improvement scheme which cleared 93 acres of central slum dwellings and replaced it with new roads and buildings, the centrepiece of which was an imposing new thoroughfare named Corporation Street, which radically altered the whole topography of central Birmingham.

There had been other examples of great provincial cities in Britain expanding and re-defining their territories and functions but none had done it over such a short period of time. And few had financed the changes *themselves*. In the late sixties and early seventies, Birmingham was earning money rapidly as 'Brummagem 'ardware' spread around the world and funds therefore were available for civic expenditure. The fact that money was cheap during the later part of the seventies, together with the territorial growth of the city and the consequent increase in rate income, enabled the initiative to be continued.

But the risks had been great and the financial houses of the City of London, largely ignored by these provincial upstarts in the Midlands, sat back and waited for the inevitable bankruptcy of the Town Council. It never came. Joe called the risk-taking 'sagacious audacity.'

On stepping down from the Mayoralty, Chamberlain entered Parliament and four years later he was in Gladstone's Cabinet as President of the Board of Trade. Just before taking up his new career in London, he wrote: 'I think I have now almost completed my municipal programme and may sing *nunc dimittis*. The Town will be parked, paved, assized, marketed, gas-and-watered and *improved* – all as the result of these three years' active work.'

So it was – and the improvements continued, albeit not at the same hectic rate. In 1890, as the exciting century was drawing to an end, the American writer J. Ralph summed it up like this: 'Birmingham is the best governed city in the world.'

It was a little difficult for a young boy to see the Birmingham of the World War II years in quite this way. Austerity cloaked the city, as it did other great provincial centres throughout the land. Anxiety, too, was in the air as we all – even youngsters like me – followed the fluctuating fortunes of the Allies. Yet, it was clear that the city functioned well. True, there was no tube to be over-crowded and to break down regularly. But the yellow Corporation buses ran through the blitz and throughout the war on time, as did the clanging trams. The schools soon returned to normal after the hiatus of the evacuation months and the water that miraculously ran from our taps at the twist of a handle was, it was loudly claimed and believed, the sweetest and purist in the land.

It may seem inappropriate that, in this account of the war years of the middle of the twentieth century I should devote so much space to the happenings of the nineteenth. I can only plead that, as a young boy, I was very aware of the achievements of those civic pioneers. A strong sense of civic pride lingered on.

In 1938, Aston Park, my own personal playground, had been the setting for a great pageant that celebrated the granting of city status to Birmingham fifty years before. Around the setting of the Jacobean great house, Aston Hall, the city's history was played out in tableaux, from its beginnings as a Roman fort, through its first recording as a small village worth twenty shillings in the Domesday Book of 1086, to the present day. At my senior school in Gower Street, we were taught about the great leap forward of the city seventy years before and I became fascinated by the feat of creating huge artificial lakes in Wales and bringing the water, fresh and clear, to our kitchen taps fifty miles away. If I knew Joseph Chamberlain only as some old toff who had lived in a large house in Moseley years ago, then, at least, I was aware of his deeds. Towards the end of the war, indeed, I cycled those miles to see for myself the great reservoir in the Elan Valley, built by the energy generated by Joe's 'civic gospel.' I was thrilled by the sight and the size of the project. I remain so to this day.

Yet, by 1938, Chamberlain's great city was no Florence. The more altruistic visions of those early councillors – some of them had spoken of recreating the glories of the Italian city – had not been realised. Certainly, Corporation Street stretched through its centre, wide and straight, spanking new council house estates were being erected at its edges and Bournville showed the rest of the world what good Quaker philanthropy could do to house workers in practical but harmonious conditions. Industry and commerce, too, were creeping out of the depression. The Jewellery Quarter had regained some of its prosperity (too late, alas, to help my father), thousands of hammers once again clanged – in small workshops, not in bedrooms now – and large factories such as the Austin and Rover motor works began to work overtime as war threatened.

Living in Aston, however, I was well aware that most of modern Birmingham was a dirty, crowded city, with out-of-date housing and poor living conditions still the norm for many, if not most, of its inhabitants.

Uncle Alf had been born in a back-to-back house. These were relics of the post Industrial Revolution boom, when families flocked into the emerging cities from the countryside, anxious to find work in the new workshops and factories. To house them, opportunistic landlords threw up dwellings that made the most of each inch of space available so that there were no gardens, just a narrow entry to take tenants past the terraced house at the front to its hunched companion, built contiguously at the back. Smoke from a hundred thousand chimneys blackened the bricks and the few stalks of grass that incongruously poked out between the cobbles. Those houses still stood all around us in Aston in the thirties and forties. The earlier ones, of course, had crumbled but they had been rebuilt, in exactly the same way, throughout Victoria's reign.

The result was that, when war was declared, there were vast tracts of Birmingham, particularly in the inner city in areas such as Aston, that were undoubtedly slums. My parents would never for one moment admit that we lived in a slum. Nor did we, despite the fact that we had no running hot water and that taking a pee meant going to the lavatory in the garden. At least, we had a garden! But Tower Road, where we lived with my grandmother in the mid thirties, contained many back-to-back houses. Down near the bottom of Potters Hill, to which we moved in 1941, lurked Summer Lane, a nest of back-to-backs and long regarded as one of the roughest streets in Brum to which, as a little boy with brushed hair and proper shoes (not boots), I was never allowed to go. To my mother, the occupants of back-to-back houses may have been the salt of the earth but they were also dirty, ill-mannered and could be violent. This was no snobbish prejudice. She knew them because she visited their homes to collect on their penny policies every week.

There was no greater reminder of the grimy state of Birmingham than was provided by returning to it from our annual holiday. Whatever the state of the family purse and however poor his health, Dad always found the money and the energy to take the four of us away for a week by the seaside every year through the thirties. A trunk would be packed and sent on ahead, I was dressed in my only suit to travel in and we would set off for a boarding house in Southsea, Bournemouth, or North Wales. There we would paddle, dig sand castles or, in Dad's case, sit in a deckchair, smoke his pipe and read Agatha Christie. Most of all, however, on mother's instructions we would 'breath deeply now.' She seemed to have a fixation about fresh air and, I suspect, always believed that Dad could have been cured if some way could have been found for him to live on a farm in the countryside where the air was good.

It certainly wasn't good in Birmingham. Returning to the city after a week by the sea brought this home to us all. Usually, the train journey took us back through the long, black tunnel that was the entry to New Street Station. It seemed to stretch forever and the smell of sooty smoke hit us all once inside it. I used to try and hold my breath until we came out of the dark onto the platforms of the station but I never managed it and would explode and be forced to gasp in lungs full of the terrible stuff.

Smokeless fuel was a thing of the future, as indeed was central heating for most of us. As a result, a million homes burned coal in an open fire place, sending the unfiltered smoke into the sky so that, if you viewed Birmingham from the neighbouring heights of the Lickey Hills or Barr Beacon, a black pall could be seen hovering over the city. As in other big cities, the fogs of autumn and winter mixed with this malevolent halo to produce a smog that killed the elderly and sick. In the case of Birmingham, however, the emissions from thousands of chimneys were complemented by the outpourings of the factories of the Black Country, which stretched to the north west of the city. (In later years, I was in the newsroom of the Birmingham Gazette, one of Britain's oldest dailies, when the management took in for a month a journalist from New Zealand, here on a sabbatical. His first assignment was to visit the Black Country. His story began: "My God! It actually IS black!").

The Birmingham air became more directly important to the Wilcox family for a brief but uncomfortable period about half way through the war. At this time, father was sent to a convalescent home. This was a misnomer, of course, because there was no cure for consumption and convalescence presumed recovery of a sort. Nevertheless, he came back, still coughing and furious because a fellow inmate had told him to 'bugger off to Russia if you like the place so much.' Fresh air was diagnosed as the answer to his condition and he was instructed to get as much of it as possible and, more to the point, open the windows of his home throughout the day, whatever the temperature. The instructions were followed and throughout that summer and well into the winter we all sat with the parlour window open, wrapped in coats and scarves as Christmas approached.

I didn't mind the discomfort and I don't remember any of the family complaining – we would do anything to alleviate Father's condition. Mind you, *he* complained about the cold all the time and felt the whole idea was daft. But I was embarrassed when my mates called and found us muffled to the eyebrows, hunched round our fire. It was a great relief all round when Dad eventually pulled down the window, coughed, spat and said that enough was enough. Mother sighed and said that the Birmingham air was no good for anybody, anyway.

The problem of air pollution in big cities was not cured, of course, until the succession of post-war Clean Air Acts created smokeless zones. It was obviously a national problem and the grit-in-the-teeth nature of Birmingham's atmosphere was not the fault of the City Council. Even a Joe Chamberlain would have found it an intangible windmill to tilt against. What *was* the Council's responsibility, however, was the continual deterioration of the inner city. The slums in districts like Aston, Balsall Heath, Smethwick and Lozells were a hang-over from Victorian times and a constant reproach to the civic authorities. It was clear, through the twenties and thirties that another 1870's initiative was needed. But these years were those of depression and tight purse strings. Where was the money (and, unspokenly, the civic energy) to come from? Then the war ended any further speculation.

As a boy and teenager, of course, I was very much aware that living in Aston was not exactly a pastoral existence. Even when I found my first job just after the war, I was shy of admitting where I lived. The little late Victorian villas of Ettington Road were quite acceptable but that the old houses of Potters Hill, with their lack of front gardens (and not much behind), smoke blackened bricks and dark tunnels in the terraces as the "back" entrance, were a step back for the Wilcox family, there was no denying.

Yet the Hill had its charms. It was almost a self-sufficient community in terms of shopping convenience. At the top there was Taylors, a small department store selling down-market clothing and draperies, once dignified by a visit from the ukulele-playing comedian George Formby, no less, who opened one of its extensions. One of our neighbours rushed up to see him and clutched to herself her audacity in crying out to him, 'Where's your uke, George?' He actually smiled back at her, she told the world.

As recorded earlier, there was Harris's sweet shop, and Henney's the grocers. But there was also a butcher who drove a 1939 Morris 14 and was therefore, it was whispered, 'doin' too well'; Saunder's the chemist's shop with huge glass containers filled with coloured liquid in the window; a pub on the corner with Tower Road; and, incongruously set in the middle of the hill, just opposite our house, Pearce's the grain merchant. This agricultural establishment had no place in the middle of an industrialised city, but it seemed to do well enough and I can see now old Mr Pearce, with his Hardyian gaiters gathering in his corduroys, stacking his hay bales behind the green doors leading to his rear yard. The smell of straw was pervasive but not unpleasant and was what I presumed to be the country smell.

At the bottom of the hill our street met the big, bustling thoroughfare of Newtown Row, near to the dreaded Summer Lane. It housed a real shopping centre – The House that Jack Built – and a score of individual shops that meandered southwards. Through the Row threaded the number 6 tram that took you straight into the heart of the city for.... what was it? Twopence or threepence? Here too was Aston Hippodrome, a second line variety theatre it must be admitted, but where once Nellie Wallace and Max Miller had starred and Laurel and Hardy were to perform. When the latter played the Hippodrome after the war, they stayed at Barton's Arms, a big ogre of a Victorian gin palace, situated just opposite the theatre and which somehow survived all the destruction of the war and the ravages of post-war reconstruction and now squats at the side of the motorway into town, like some disapproving old widow. Its interior has been lovingly refurbished to recreate the days of its youth and it now has the reputation of being a very fine gastropub.

There was, then, plenty of character as well as dirt about Potters Hill. The Hill, however, was too steep and just too busy for children to play on it and through the war years I would walk or bicycle back down to Ettington Road to link up with Baden to play. Doodle bugs never reached the Midlands and, after the bombing of the early years, it was quite safe for children of our age to play in streets like Ettington, for there were few cars – and none parked at the kerbside, of course. And paedophilia, it seems, had not been invented then.

Before football and cricket took hold in our teens, we used every physical characteristic of our environment to create our own fictional landscape. Opposite Baden's house at number 66, the roadway had once been dug up, leaving a slight mound of tarmacadam patching stretching across the road from one pavement to the other. This became the bridge on which Little John had met Robin Hood, with neither giving way until a fight with staves ended with Robin plunging into the river. It was a waste of time me proclaiming that because my name was John, I should win. Baden was bigger, so it was always me who was knocked into the water.

It was possible, then, to have a warm, safe upbringing in Birmingham during the war years once the bombing had ended, and I wallowed in the love of my family and the fun to be had with my friends in the grimy back streets. Yet I was conscious as I grew into my teens that the city had fallen away from the high standards set all those years ago by the City Fathers and that it was over-crowded, contained far too many slum properties, and needed another Great Leap Forward.

That came years later when, as the Municipal Correspondent of the Birmingham Gazette, I observed it as first hand – or, at least, I watched the planning of it. The Manzoni Plan (he was the City Engineer and became Sir Herbert as a result of his work) was tabled in the early fifties in the Council Chamber and put into practice over the next decade. The city centre was gutted and a network of flyovers and pedestrian underpasses installed. Areas like Potters Hill and Tower Road completely disappeared and in their places reared tower blocks. It was a disaster. The under-passes added to the difficulties of elderly and unfit pedestrians and also became places of crime. The high rise flats lacked local amenities and exterminated the community spirit of places like Potters Hill.

Birmingham, of course, was not the only city to suffer in this way. Ugly architectural modernism and arrogant social planning typified post war development all across the country. Now, hopefully, the damage is being righted. The Second City has had another go at its centre, tearing out the old Bull Ring and installing breath-taking buildings that have earned the approval of architectural critics and the public alike. The new concert hall is now worthy of a city which first gave Mendelssohn's 'Elijah' to the world and the Royal Ballet has made its home in Birmingham. There are still black spots, of course – particularly in districts like Aston, Lozells and Handsworth – but the only back to-back houses still standing have been mothballed and presented as museum pieces to show how bad it once was. What has also changed, however, is the air of social calm that we inhabited during the war. Ethnic ghettoes have produced race riots and gang killings, far worse now than the sooty air and grimy buildings that I remember depressing me when I was young.

I guess I was lucky, after all.

Chapter 5

"THE SECOND CASUALTY OF WAR"

S omeone once wrote: 'If the first casualty of war is truth, then the second must surely be education.' More than 20,000 teachers left their profession during World War II to join the services. They left behind them a gap that was filled, or rather partially filled, with men and women who were called out of retirement, part time teachers, usually women, who were urged to become full time, and elderly practitioners who were nearing the end of their careers. The result was overcrowded classes and a decline in teaching standards.

Until recently, I always regarded myself as a casualty of those circumstances. That gap in the autumn of 1939, when Baden and I saw most of our classmates evacuated and our school closed down, may have been blissful for us at the time, but it flattened the learning curve of this late developer and set back my education at a critical time. The hole-in-the-corner classes at Mrs Johnson's that followed did little to penetrate my brain and the bombing of 1940, when I remember dozing off in class after nights on those awful benches, left me blinking with incomprehension at the end of the school day.

When then, in 1942, the dreaded eleven plus examination arrived, I didn't know my long division from a multiple fraction. I couldn't recall any formulae because my brain had not recorded any of them in the first place. Pi to me was something you ate. On the other hand, I had learned to read at a precociously young age and history and geography were of genuine interest. But arithmetic, or mathematics as I was beginning dimly to call it, was not only a closed book, it was locked and sealed. As best I remember, the non-numerate sections of the eleven plus examination were easy enough, but I just sat and stared at the arithmetic questions, hardly answering one. Consequently, I did not just fail the test, I plummeted.

Today, perhaps, the examiners might have shown some flexibility in dealing with such a lopsided paper. But the Old Guard were very much in charge in 1942 and evidence of such startling innumeracy could not be contemplated, even if the handling of the other subjects showed promise. If you couldn't do sums, you couldn't go to grammar school. So I did not.

Understandably, this disappointed and depressed my parents. My father shook his head, indulged in a bout of coughing and said, in only half-mocking tones: 'Oh lord. My son is a failure.' I hated that (and still do). My disgrace was mitigated to some extent, however, by the fact that, amazingly, Baden failed as well. This was truly surprising because he was a bright boy in class, whereas I just tried to hide. But together we went with the other failures, plus those no-hopers who had not sat the examination, to Gower Street Senior School, in Lozells, a district then as now even less salubrious than Aston.

Schooldays in these early years of the war were strongly influenced, of course, by air raid precautions. Luckily, Birmingham experienced relatively few daylight bombing attacks and we rarely had to put into practice the drill of filing into the roughly built concrete shelters that had been erected in the playground. Gas mask carrying, however, was *de rigueur.* The whole population was issued with these strange fitments, consisting of short, cylindrical chemical filters attached to a face mask which allowed visibility of a sort through a celluloid screen, the whole held in place by rubber straps that fitted over the head (and painfully caught in the hair). The smell of the rubber and whatever was in the cylinders made the wearing of these things most unpleasant, not least because the inside of the celluloid would mist up so that it became virtually impossible to see. Only later did we learn to wipe a smear of soap on the screen to stop the misting, although this did little to improve visibility. We were solemnly told that, in the event of being caught in a gas attack without our gas masks, we should take out our handkerchiefs, pee on them and tie them around our mouths. We all grinned. The rude boys asked if we could have a rehearsal but the request was refused. The masks were carried in a little cardboard box, slung from the shoulder by string so that the box bumped on your bottom as you walked. Forgetting to take your gas mask to school was a caning offence and I was beaten for this crime. It was, I think, about 1942 before the rule was relaxed and we were allowed to leave the unpleasant, pigs'-snout masks to gather dust at home.

Given that our future depended crucially upon the outcome of the war, it might be thought that we would have had lessons, perhaps as part of a current affairs curriculum, on the state of the campaigns overseas: in the Western Desert, Malaya and Burma, the Pacific and, in later years, Europe. But I recall none of that; no teaching to explain what the war was all about; no unpickings of the theory of fascism or National Socialism. Perhaps this was too much to expect from a state school, but we were not too young (it was, after all, a *senior* school) and many of us were not too stupid to have developed a keen interest in the great issues of the day. Those special lessons, too, given to the senior forms, on the history of Birmingham's civic development and which so excited my interest, showed that the school authorities were not slavishly restricted to a three R's syllabus.

By the same token, there was no school play nor any stimulus to spark our interest in the arts, except a weekly music lesson where it was found, to my surprise, that I had a pleasant singing voice that led me to join the choir at St Paul's Church, Lozells, now, in the twenty first century, a centre for Muslim community activities. We did have a fortnightly treat, however, when a creaky film projector was set up and we were allowed to watch a film. Unfortunately, they were all boring silent documentaries from the early twenties. The one exception I remember was a showing of Griffiths's 'The Birth of a Nation,' which I would now give my eye teeth to see again, but the flickering, grainy print of which, in 1942, evoked only derisory cries from the hooligans in the back seats. For some reason, the film show was an occasion when these lads would take in raw vegetables, carrots, parsnips, swedes and so on to chew. It became a ritual for them, but to me these uncooked, indigestible roots were no substitute for the choc ices and Mars bars of cherished memory.

Perhaps the most surprising missing element from the war time school curriculum, however, was that of organised games playing and coaching. We had physical training, of a sort, in the school hall (a back street school like Gower Street, of course, would never boast a gymnasium) but no games of football or cricket under tuition. There was never any question of playing on grass, anyway, but no doubt one of the reasons for the omission was the absence of young, fit teachers to oversee the activity and to coach us.

As the war against Germany, Italy and Japan began slowly to swing in favour of the Allies, the boys of Gower Street School, were subjected to a series of patriotic appeals for money: Warship Week, Wings for Victory and so on. We were urged to bring in cash and each class was encouraged to compete to see who could raise the most money. Good for the war effort, no doubt, but another drain on families such as mine with poor incomes and sometimes I did not relay the request home, dropping my head and avoiding the teacher's eye when collection time came round.

Throughout those years I stayed humiliatingly bottom of the class in mathematics, which remained too heavy an imbalance to offset my reasonable performance in the arts subjects, particularly in English, where I was even beginning to shine. Lacking, however, any real personality, distinction in class or confidence, I was moving inexorably towards quitting school at fourteen – then the leaving age – and scrabbling around to find a job… doing what? I had not the faintest idea but I knew it would have to be, by definition, uninteresting and dead-ended: in a factory, perhaps (although I had no digital dexterity), or as a clerk or, horror of horrors, serving in a shop. The future looked black and I felt frustrated, a failure who was letting down his family.

Then, just before the D-Day landings of 1944, when I was thirteen, I was thrown a lifeline – one which was to change my life.

I was told that it was possible at my age to sit an entrance examination for Aston Commercial School. This offered further education up to the age of sixteen, the conventional Grammar School leaving age. No fees to be paid, although my family would have to buy a basic number of books and, if the smart brown and blue school uniform was out of reach (it was!), a school tie and a badge for my jacket. I knew the school well. It was situated in Whitehead Road, at the junction with Ettington Road; an impressive, stylish edifice of yellow stone, with even the look of a French chateau about it, although I was not to realise this resemblance until later. Baden and I knew the schoolcaretaker, and he often allowed the two of us and our friends to play in the school playground during the holidays.

It was co-educational, with a weighting of two to one in favour of girls and, to be honest, it was best suited for the training of secretaries and book-keepers. But its syllabus included French and notably, shorthand. This was important to me because I knew that journalism, one of the only professions still conceivably open to badly educated duffers like me, demanded this skill and I had developed a hopeless ambition that, one day, I might earn my living by writing. This was an out-of-the-blue opportunity to begin climbing the steep ladder leading to the achievement of that ambition, for newspaper reporters wrote, didn't they? And they wore trench raincoats and snap brimmed trilbies; better, a hundred times better, than working in a shop. But first loomed the dreaded entrance examination. I was told that it was stiff and, of course, there was the prospect – no, the near certainty – that I would muff the mathematics paper and ruin my chances.

To my joy, Baden, who had remained my best friend throughout our years at Gower Street, also applied to take the examination and we settled down to work hard towards it. We sat it together, as the Allied troops were inching their way inland from the bloody Normandy beaches, and, to my amazement, I passed. (I always knew Baden would, for he could do sums – it was surely a fluke that he had failed the eleven plus.) I remember that I wrote what I felt was a particularly good essay and doddled through the history and geography papers, coming up hard, once again of course against the damned sums. Yet I finished that paper somehow, even tackling the algebra section with some sort of logic. I was through!

Yet, as I waited through the summer holidays of 1944 to attend my new school, I still expected a letter to arrive saying that it had all been a mistake and that my papers had somehow been mixed with those of another boy. In the first week of school that threat still hung over me and when, to my astonishment, I was voted by my classmates to become Form Captain, I knew I was doomed. The Form Master, white-haired Mr Emmott, nodded when I was proposed for the job (to this day I still don't know why, because I had not exactly shone in those first few days and, apart from Baden, I only knew one other boy in the class). He said that he would have to look at my entrance examination papers to make sure that I was bright enough to justify the honour. This surely meant that he would see that my maths were pathetic and jettison me – and even throw me out of the school. Oh, the humiliation that was to come! But it never arrived. Nothing more was said and I had my foot on the first rung of that ladder at last.

Over the next three years, as the war came to its weary conclusion, I blossomed in the warm atmosphere of that fine school, in an ambiance where talent was allowed to bloom and ambition encouraged to train for jobs far more demanding than secretaries and book keepers. As Headmaster, we had Dr W. Flack, a distinguished mathematician who introduced to the syllabus such esoteric subjects as debating and public speaking. There was a thriving dramatic society, an equally active School Parliament and, most blessed of gifts to young boys, a fine gymnasium with a sports master who supervised coaching in football, cricket and boxing (the girls were equally looked after in terms of netball, hockey and tennis). We also had our own playing fields, a twenty minute walk away in Perry Barr.

From being a surly, back-of-the-classroom boy, living with a constant fear of being singled out for humiliation, I gradually acquired confidence and even leadership skills. After three years, I ended as School Captain; Secretary of the Dramatic Society (also taking the lead in the annual school play); Prime Minister in the School Parliament (Labour, of course); winner of the cup for public speaking; left half in the school football first XI; and vice captain (under my still best friend and terrifyingly fast bowler, Baden) in the cricket XI. I managed to get my certificate for 140 words per minute at shorthand and came top in the final examinations in English, History and Geography. With inevitable consistency, however, I came a resounding bottom in Mathematics. But by then I didn't care – well, not too much, anyway.

More importantly than all of the above, however, I discovered girls. Gower Street, of course, had been a boys only school and, as a shy lad with plenty to be shy about, I had always regarded the opposite sex with caution, if not downright suspicion. The conditions imposed by the war – restrictions on travel, the blackout, the closing down of many clubs in the early days – contributed to an absence of formal opportunities for communication and understanding. As puberty stole up on me, girls became just another potential source of humiliation.

At the ACS, however, we were thrust into proximity. Not close, but close enough to break down the fear. The classes were not mixed but the extra mural activities were. It was impossible to be shy of a girl when you bounced lines off her in the school play, or debated with her in the school parliament. (Why, I pondered, did all the pretty ones have to be Conservative?) So I fell in love, quite frequently, in fact, and always without declaring my devotion. But more importantly, I also made friends with girls and discovered that I liked their company. This was made easier because of Baden, who had black curly hair, had reached the height of six feet by the time he was fifteen and had all the confidence in the world. In his shade, then, I began to pull – in a strictly innocent, chaste way, of course.

It was, then, quite appropriate that I should complete my sexual emancipation many years later by marrying a girl from the ACS. Betty Longfield and I never met at school – she is two and half years older – but we met on the committee of the old scholar's association after I had left the school. We have been together ever since.

The removal of the gender barriers at Aston was helped by the introduction of Farming Camp School. Dr Flack, ever the innovator (he was later to introduce dancing classes for both sixth forms), had decided mid-way through the war years that the older pupils would benefit – as would the war effort – by spending a month of the summer term working on the land deep in rural Warwickshire, living under canvas. The idea was that the children in the fourth, fifth and sixth forms would spend the mornings doing conventional school work and the afternoons doing unskilled but back-breaking work picking potatoes, strawberries and the like on local farms. Our bucolic environment entered into our formal school work in the shape of projects on the natural world and rural culture. For some reason I chose to become an expert on the Women's Institute and also, perhaps more appropriately, the elm tree. When Dutch elm disease struck the countryside decades later, I felt personally bereaved.

We lived in a field at Bidford, near Stratford-upon-Avon, ate our meals and sat in lessons in wooden sheds and slept, in groups of six, in old army bell tents, the girls on one side of the field, the boys on the other, never the twain to meet after lights out.

Except that they did, once in 1946, when an expedition set out from the boys' tents after dark, worming its way across the grass on its stomach, like Commandos, to reach the girls' tents and a warm welcome – of cakes and lemonade. The excitement, however, was too much for some of the girls, whose giggling awoke members of the staff and all was discovered. Disgrace ensued for the members of the expedition, who included Baden. I was not in the party, not because I was afraid of discovery (although I was not at all sure what I would have done on reaching the Promised Land on the other side of the field) but because Baden had won the affection of my then girl friend, the magnificent Jean Cook, and I had no-one 'to visit.' The result was that when, a year later, the school captaincy had to be decided and the choice was between Baden and myself, I clinched it by a hair's breadth, because I hadn't, in the Headmaster's phrase, 'broken trust' the previous year. I felt like a fraud for months afterwards.

We were at Farming Camp School when the news of the dropping of the atom bomb on Hiroshima was announced. One of the boys in my tent had a portable radio and, long after lights out, we gathered round it, attempting to comprehend what we were hearing. The newsreel footage of the evil cloud, climbing into the heavens like some diseased and swollen mushroom, had not then been released – not that we could have seen it anyway, locked as we were miles from the nearest cinema – so that it was hard to visualise the enormity of this first weapon of mass destruction.

'It's just a bloody big bomb, isn't it?' asked Norman Wood, the green light from the radio dial reflected on his face in the darkness of the tent. 'Just a bomb only bigger. That's all it is.'

It wasn't, of course, it was the end of the war. We had all been led to believe that the end of hostilities against Germany in May 1945, was only the first stage. The war against Japan would continue and it would take months, if not years, to leapfrog across the islands of the Pacific until the final, costly attack on the Japanese mainland. Now, to us boys lying in our sleeping tents in a field in Warwickshire, it gradually became clear that the 'bloody big bomb' in fact heralded the end of World War II.

It was at about this time that my family visited me at Farming Camp School. Dad arrived wrapped in blankets, in the back of the old Ford, which had been disinterred with the relaxation of petrol rationing and driven down by an old friend. Mother and my sister Margaret came too and I felt hugely embarrassed by all of the fuss caused as he was allowed, by special dispensation, to be driven across the field to my tent and then lowered onto a folding chair outside it. He looked close to death, with sunken cheeks and waxen complexion. I learned later that he felt it would be the last time he would see me and insisted on leaving his bed and being driven down to Bidford.

He died, in fact, several weeks later, in his bed at Potters Hill, after my return. He had fought the disease that, literally, consumed him with courage and humour for most of my lifetime and had lived to see my partial rehabilitation from my failed state as a pupil and, more importantly, the end of the war. But his own battle could never be won, of course, and he told Mother shortly before he died that this time, he was 'just too tired.' He died on 18th August 1945 – my mother's 50th birthday – at the age of 52, leaving a huge gap in the lives of all of us who knew and loved him.

The dropping of The Bomb and the death of my father seemed to bring to an end a discrete section of my life, although I had two more years left of my formal education at the ACS. Behind me were the war years, the sickness that hung over our family as a constant reminder of mortality and my own poor performance in the classroom and consequent lack of self-worth. Before me lay those first steps on the ladder that were to lead, many, many rungs later, to publication as a novelist and the eventual diagnosis that my inability to make $13 + 7 = 23$ (ah! – sorry, 22) was not stupidity but an affliction called dyscalculia, the numerate version of dyslexia.

I must add a coda to those happy wartime days at Aston Commercial School. Betty and I paid it a visit about fifteen years ago, after our abortive trip to find Uncle Alf's grave. Then, as now, the building looked the same from the outside but we knew the interior would be completely changed, for it had long since ceased being a specialist school and had become Holte Grammar School. We hung around outside the familiar steps leading to the entrance, wondering whether it was better to turn away, for we knew that we would not find the same spirit within, after forty years, and we did not wish to court disappointment.

As we dithered, a youngish man came through the door, ushering out a visitor. He asked if he could help us and we explained, half-heartedly, that we were walking down memory lane but didn't wish to bother anyone and would be on our way. No, no, he insisted. Allow him to say good-bye to his guest and he would show us round the school. We were invited to wait inside, 'by the fish tank in the wall.' Fish tank!

He was, it ensued, the headmaster and he devoted the next hour to taking us round. Of course things had changed. The pupils wore blue and white instead of brown and blue and every single face was either brown or black. Each desk seemed to house a computer screen and there was a great deal of extra equipment in the gymnasium. But the enthusiasm of the headmaster and his delight in his school sat completely in the tradition of the great Flack. And the faces that greeted us in every classroom were alert and smiling.

We left feeling very happy.

Then, in 2007, we made a second, deliberately briefer, pilgrimage. The school was now teaching seven to eight year olds as the "Aston Campus" of a large comprehensive called The Broadway School. Litter surrounded the exterior and a coat of paint was much needed. Rumours, we heard, were rife that the fine old building was due to be pulled down in a couple of years time. We left this time feeling considerably less happy.

Chapter 6

MOON OVER MIAMI

After my father, the two greatest influences on my life during my war-time growing up years were the public library in Aston's Albert Road and Hollywood, in far away California. More of the library later, for it was American films that took a more immediate hold. It's a shameful thing to admit – how much more impressive to nominate an inspiring teacher (as did Emlyn Williams with his Miss Cooke, so producing 'The Corn is Green,') but I was not that lucky and, young Philistine that I was, it would have taken a completely charismatic figure to have outshone the screen and influenced more the way I thought and behaved.

For years, I believed that all cars throughout the world (with the exception of our very special, pre-war Ford 8) had a gear shift sticking out of the steering column, parallel to the floor, and that Clive of India spoke with an American accent and looked like Tyrone Power. I reasoned that the smart women I saw on Saturday mornings in the centre of Birmingham, when mother took me for an ice cream at Lewis's department store, didn't have long, curling eye lashes like Joan Crawford only because our city was backward and provincial. And I became convinced that a John Wayne punch was the way to solve most complex issues.

American films, with their simple plots, glamorous stars, strange and sumptuous backdrops and crisp dialogue, became my release from the miseries of the war, my father's illness and the dread of maths lessons. I managed to scrape enough money – there was precious little else to spend it on, anyway – to visit the Orient in High Street Aston, or the Odeon, Perry Barr, once or sometimes even twice a week. As a result, I swallowed Hollywood's precepts and standards whole and adopted them as my own.

Louis B. Meyer's sentimentality, oozing with virtues of motherhood and family life, as evinced most regularly in MGM's Andy Hardy series, became mine. I came to believe, as did Cecil B. de Mille, that ten red-coated Mounties appearing over a rise could subdue a valley-full of Indians, and that it would never occur to a band of Apaches, attacking John Ford's Stagecoach, to shoot the lead horses and so bring the thing to a stop. I accepted completely the filmic view of romance: that, despite perhaps the odd wobble, everyone was destined to fall in love, marry and live happily ever after. There was certainly no sex before marriage because it was never hinted at in the films I saw, except in the case of certain fallen women, who were to be pitied. The American Hayes Code, introduced in the early thirties to clean up Hollywood, ensured that, even when married couples were filmed in bed, the man must always have one foot on the floor. The great unspoken dictum was that you married and only *then* was sex, one of life's great mysteries, satisfactorily opened up to you – rather like getting a sweet (perhaps even a choc ice!) for being good.

Of course I was reading throughout the war years, but books lacked the visual intensity of the cinema and only later did I attain the intellectual stamina to tackle the great novels and realise that their values were superior to those of Hollywood. Similarly, the theatre was expensive and more-or-less out of my reach. And when I did visit the Birmingham Repertory, the Theatre Royal or the Alexandra, I found the plays artificial and remote. No, it was films for me: available, infinitely glamorous and completely engulfing.

I write that films were available, yet not completely so for children. A licensing system meant that films during the war were graded A (for adults) U for under fourteens and H for horror films. Entry to the latter was denied for children under fourteen, whether accompanied or not. The A's could be seen by children under that age only if accompanied by adults, but children could attend the U's unaccompanied. This system, however, was not going to stop a cinemaniac like me. If an A film took my fancy – something containing Cagney-type violence, for instance – I would wait outside the cinema, money in hand, until a likely, sympathetic looking adult came along and agreed to take me in. This backfired on me once when, having been given my ticket at the kiosk by my friendly adult, I visited the lavatory before entering the auditorium. Arriving at the entrance alone, I was accosted by a truculent usherette.

'Ere,' she said, 'you're not over fourteen.'

'Yes I am.'

'Right, then. What year were you born?'

'I… er… nineteen… er…' Never did I hate my incompetence at arithmetic more than at that moment. I just couldn't work out my fictional date of birth. I stood on one leg, floundering, until she took pity on me and let me in.

The men and women up there on the screen mostly never deviated from basic types. The heroes, for instance, were rarely introspective, thoughtful men who might have doubts on a course of action. (A possible exception to this rule was the monosyllabic Gary Cooper, but even a boy couldn't avoid the thought that his hesitation was probably due to difficulty in remembering his lines). They were strong, rugged, brave and knew exactly what to do in any difficult situation. Of course, there were other, more introspective leading men such as Ronald Colman, Leslie Howard and William Powell who never punched anyone, but to me they seemed to be effete aberrations who appeared mainly in 'women's pictures.' The real kings of the screen to my eyes were he-men. Spencer Tracey, Clark Gable, Errol Flynn, Randolph Scott, Humphrey Bogart, Cagney and the great Wayne typified the breed. Confronted by a problem their first and usually only reaction was to fight. And could they fight! These men had fists of concrete.

Some of them could even act.

On the other hand, the requirement for a leading lady was beauty, not acting skills. How someone like Bette Davis, whose pop-out eyes, non-stop smoking and mannered voice I hated, could win two Oscars amazed me. No, I grovelled at the high heels of Greer Garson, Linda Darnell, Anne Sheridan and Laraine Day, ladies whose wrap-around teeth sparkled like diamonds but whose acting was usually one-dimensional.

To a boy in the monochrome Britain of the early forties, they were goddesses – and none more so than my first and lasting love, Betty Grable, from St Louis, Missouri, who was five foot something of completely artificial perfection. She had hair of spun gold, luscious lips that were always cherry red, more curves than the French Corniche and legs that started under her armpits and went on for ever. I lost myself to her at the age of ten when I am convinced my voice broke half way through *Moon Over Miami*. The film was awful but she was in it and I was entranced. She usually appeared in trite musicals (*Down Argentina Way, Coney Island, Mother Wore Tights* etc) and she could hoof a little and sing rather less than adequately, but it didn't matter. She looked as though you could take a spoon and scoop her off the Technicoloured screen and eat her. She became the most famous pin-up for American troops during the war (our chaps had Vera Lynn, for goodness sake!) and inspired several armies. She certainly inspired me and a part of my youth went with her when she died in 1973.

The great strength of Hollywood during the war (and before and after it, for that matter) was the studio system, with its raft of type-cast actors. It provided a safe predictability and continuity for both the stars and the studios that employed them. From Warner Brothers, then, you could rely on hard-nosed gangster films, with Cagney, Bogart and Edward G. Robinson; M.G.M. for sentimental dramas, adorned by Garbo, Garson and Shearer; Twentieth Century Fox for lush musicals sparkling with Grable, Alice Faye and Tyrone Power; and Paramount for comedies starring Crosby and Hope or epics with Cooper, Ray Milland and Paulette Goddard. The stars themselves sometimes struggled against, but usually wallowed in vehicles that were crafted for their particular strengths, so that they rarely had to extend their range: Cooper, Henry Fonda, and Wayne in westerns; Bette Davis and Garson in weepies; Clark Gable and Tracey in action pictures; and Flynn, definitively, in swashbuckling roles.

Sometimes the system slipped out of gear. Bette Davis, whose intelligence I grew to respect once I was out of short trousers, rebelled against type casting in the late thirties and fled to Britain in search of more testing roles. She was sued by Warners Brothers and forced to limp back to Hollywood and accept the roles offered her – but she dug in and got better stuff and her two Oscars. Flynn, whom God created only to wear tights and swing a sword, was a dismal Soames in a remake of the Edwardian drawing room family classic, *The Forsyte Saga* and – horror of horrors – it is rumoured that James Cagney was considered at one time for casting in the Flynn part in that greatest of swashbucklers, *The Adventures of Robin Hood*... Imagine a 5ft 3ins Robin of Sherwood with a Bronx accent!

The inbred nature of type casting in Hollywood's greatest years is best summed up by the (I do hope not apocryphal) story that crept out of America when Ronald Reagan was first mooted as a possible President of the United States. Reagan had been a Warner Brothers contract player for years, never making star billing and usually featured as a Flynn buddy in a succession of westerns. Jack Warner, the old boss of the studio, was on his deathbed when the news reached him that Reagan was considering running. Jack raised a wavering hand and exclaimed, 'No, no. Flynn for president. Reagan for best friend...'

My interest in cinema deepened the more films I saw and I began pursuing the great icons of the past. I jumped on the re-release of *The Gold Rush*, with its new music and sound track spliced on by Chaplin and I appreciated for the first time the little man's artistry. More difficult to find were traces of Douglas Fairbanks's work. But somehow I tracked down a showing of the silent *The Black Pirate* (1924) and realised who had shown Flynn how to swash a buckle. (Long, long after the war, Betty and I had dinner in a small back street restaurant in Brighton. Sitting at the next table was Margaret Johnston, a middle-ranking English actress of the fifties, her very elderly American husband, and one other man. I couldn't quite overhear their conversation but it gradually dawned on me that Johnston's husband was the man – Parker, I have not been able to trace his first name – who had actually directed the great Fairbanks in The Black Pirate. That evening I felt that a little bit of stardust from the great days of Hollywood had drifted onto our table.)

It would be wrong to think that our cinema screens during the war were filled only by American imports, although they must have accounted for at least 95 per cent of the films we saw then. In many ways, the small British film industry had its best years during this time.

Alfred Hitchcock and Alexander Korda had emerged during the thirties as directors/impresarios quite able to hold their own with Hollywood, and the British stage, of course, had long provided America with impeccably trained actors who went on to make huge reputations and long careers in California: George Arliss, who won the third Oscar, after its inception in 1929, for Best Actor, Ronald Colman, Charles Laughton, Gladys Cooper, May Whitty, Greer Garson, Donald Crisp, Cedric Hardwick, David Niven, C. Aubrey Smith, Herbert Marshall, Merle Oberon and, of course, Stan Laurel and the great Chaplin. The thirties had also seen a series of low budget, home-produced films that became popular 'fillers' for the Odeons and Gaumont cinemas that straddled the country. In fact, the top box office star in Britain for the last three years before the war was the gormless Lancashire comedian, George Formby – he who had so impressed our neighbour when he came to Potters Hill – who never made a Hollywood film in his life. It was, however, the growing realisation by the war time British government that films were a most potent form of propaganda that gave the home industry its great fillip.

The British had been slow to realise the potential of film in whipping up patriotic support for war. In the early months of World War I, the British government placed a virtual ban on war correspondents, photographers and moving picture cameramen operating in or near the front line. Yet it recognised the surging popularity of the moving pictures and it encouraged the setting up of makeshift cinemas to offer shows to the troops, often within sound of the German guns. By mid-1916, there were twenty such cinemas operating in the British sector and one boasted an orchestra of eight musicians. In 1917, the British had accepted the power of the screen and the Government commissioned W.G. Griffith, the greatest film maker in America (he created 'The Birth of a Nation,' the early classic that, in the Second World War, had failed to impress my turnip-eating classmates) to make a propaganda film. The great man visited the front with a team, including stars Lillian and Dorothy Gish, and shot his epic, The Hearts of the World, mainly in Britain and California – the front line, he confessed later, was 'lacking in visual impact.' So too, it proved, was the final film.

Both the Germans and the Americans, after their entry into the war in 1917, were far more enterprising in their use of films as propaganda. When U35 set out from the Adriatic port of Cattaro on 26th July 1916, its captain, Lothar von Arnauld de la Periere, took with him a cameraman. Within three weeks, the film man had recorded the sinking of 54 merchantmen, grossing 91,000 tons, the most successful voyage undertaken by a submarine on either side. His moving images of torpedoes exploding, ships sinking bows up beneath the waves and survivors being taken on board the U boat, were shown around the world, giving the impression that Germany was winning the sea war.

The embryonic Hollywood rushed to turn out films to help the American war effort. Chaplin (assuaging his guilt, it was said, at not returning to Britain to fight at the front) and Fairbanks made shorts to help the War Bonds drives and Mary Pickford resisted rape by an Austrian soldier in the tear jerker, The Little American.

It was the German director Leni Riefenstahl, however, who created probably the greatest propaganda movie of all time when, in 1934, she undertook a personal commission from Hitler to chronicle the Nazi Party rally in Nuremberg. The images she recorded of the huge flags hanging around the ampitheatre, the thousands of arms raised in the Nazi salute and the choruses of *seigheil!* revealed to the world for the first time the power of Nazi Germany. It was a creative and frightening piece of work, which she repeated two years later in covering the Berlin Olympic Games.

When World War II broke out in 1939, then, the concept of films as a potent means of conveying propaganda was well established and even the British were prepared for it – well, more or less…! The pioneering work of John Grierson in making high quality documentaries for specific commercial purposes in the thirties (*Night Mail, Coal Face*) had impressed the Government to the point that a national film unit was set up to make shorts starring one of Grierson's protégés, the lugubrious Humphrey Jennings, and encouraging the populace *inter alia,* to save paper, Dig for Victory, and go easy on the tap water.

To a young teenager with a love of films, these shorts to me were travesties of the filmmakers' art. What I found more interesting was to see the way that the commercial studios rallied to the flag to make pictures that contained a more subtle patriotic message, one that was subtly wrapped in an exciting but believable story. And there were plenty of them from British studios: *Convoy, Target for Tonight, One of Our Aircraft is Missing, 49th Parallel, The Life and Death of Colonel Blimp, The Foreman Went to France* etc. Probably the best of them all came late in the war, when Laurence Olivier was encouraged to make *Henry V,* as an allegory showing the plucky British at Agincourt fighting and succeeding against overwhelming odds. Who better a propagandist than the Bard himself?

There were three commercial films produced in Britain at different times in the war, however, which were particularly effective in conveying the propaganda message in the gentlest and most plausible fashion. They featured stories about each of the three services and they were under-stated in the best British manner, comparing well with the more strident films emerging from Hollywood at this time.

The first, made in 1942 and starring Noel Coward, who also wrote the script and co-directed with the young David Lean, was based on the story of HMS Kelly, the bombed destroyer commanded by Coward's friend Lord Louis Mountbatten. *In Which We Serve* was a typical Coward creation: it presented snapshots in the style of *Cavalcade* and *This Happy Breed* of gutsy Cockneys getting on with the war at sea and on the home front. Viewed today it creaks and groans rather. There is one risible scene in which Coward, as the captain of the newly commissioned destroyer, addresses his crew on deck. Hands deep in jacket pockets, his cap at the most camp and jaunty angle, Coward (who had himself experienced a most embarrassingly short stay in the army in World War I) asks: 'Some of you have served with me before. What kind of ship do I want?' A young rating raises his hand and in the tones of Mayfair replies, 'A heppy ship, sah. A heppy ship.' Nevertheless, the film has stirring action sequences, good performances – particularly one by Richard Attenborough in his first film – and it does not demonise the enemy.

These qualities are present also in the other two distinguished examples of the genre. *The Way to the Stars* plays down the action for an introspective, thoughtful analysis of what it was like to be in an RAF squadron when aircrew were being lost by the week – a kind of *Dawn Patrol* or *Journey's End* without the histrionics. The portrayals of Michael Redgrave and John Mills in the lead roles could not have been further from the heroics of Hollywood leading men: withdrawn, understated and sensitive. *The Way Ahead,* made in 1944, shows no action at all and recounts the way in which a young officer, David Niven, trains a diverse group of conscripted rookie soldiers to face the reality of warfare. The film fades out as the platoon is entrenched in Tunisia, rifles levelled on the parapet, in its first action, waiting for the Germans to approach across the plain. Niven, who had left Hollywood in 1939 to come back to fight, was a serving Lieutenant Colonel at the time and had been granted leave to act in the film. For me, it is the best of the three.

So, indeed, the British film industry came of age during the war, gaining confidence from Government support and greatly increased earnings from the millions who were now flocking to the cinemas. It continued to make stiff upper lip service dramas long after the war, often featuring John Mills, on the conning tower of a submarine or behind the wheel of a desert truck. And I loved them all. Perhaps, in fact, it was the more honest and believable approach taken by the Brits to their subject matter during the war that made me look, towards the end, with a more critical eye to the rock-fist attitude of the American heroes. Or perhaps I was just growing up.

Certainly, Hollywood provided enough commercial propaganda films for the British market during the war. If the British were better at reflecting the *real* agonies of warfare, there was no gainsaying that the Americans made magnificent gung-ho war films, where the enemy were bastards and the Yanks were heroes to the last reel. *Wake Island, Bataan, Thirty Seconds Over Tokyo, They Were Expendable, Edge of Darkness* and the *Purple Heart* were all good examples. I thrilled to them all.

I did not, however, thrill to *Mrs Miniver,* even though it won an Academy Award for one of my goddesses, Greer Garson. The problem was that I didn't know any British housewife like that: always arranging vases of roses, hair impeccable, and married to that great lump of a feller, Walter Pidgeon. (At about this time I was beginning to think that Garson was a bit too old for me – and, anyway, what would the luscious B. Grable think about it all?) The sentimentality of the plot (typical MGM) jarred with me and, even at the age of eleven, I found it implausible.

As the war went on and the memory of Coventry and the bombing began to recede a little, I found it difficult again to hate the Germans. No revelations about the persecution of the Jews had yet leaked out, of course, and I returned to my original feeling that they couldn't be *that* bad, could they? When Ann Sheridan in occupied Norway embraced the young, *nice* German soldier who was in love with her in *Edge of Darkness* and then slipped the blade of the scissors between his ribs, I was disgusted. How would we have felt if this had happened to one of our chaps in, say, Italy?

By the same token, I was unimpressed by the sudden *volte face* of Hollywood to the Russians after the USSR entered the war. From being dull, surly figures, ripe for satirising (*Ninotchka*), they had become worthy heroes overnight, deserving of our support (*Mission to Moscow, Quiet Flows the Don*). Mind you, it didn't seem long before John Wayne was back blasting away at the Commies in *Green Beret*.

Growing up at last or just a touch sated with Hollywood's products? Both perhaps. One thing is sure, however: my love affair with the cinema continued unabated throughout the war years and, it must be acknowledged, still continues to this day. Of course, I am much more selective now – and, indeed, I feel there is a greater need to be selective now, for I don't relish being blasted out of my seat by a series of explosions and car chases. Nevertheless, the Odeon Salisbury, with its umpteen screens, can still match the magic of the visits to the Odeon in New Street, Birmingham, all those years ago.

I attach certain films to certain cinemas in my memory. *Stagecoach* and, later, *Red River* will always be associated with that central Birmingham Odeon. And its name-sake in Perry Bar conjures up the frightening fight with the giant squid in *Reap the Wild Wind*. *A Guy Called Joe* is linked indelibly to my local, the Orient, in High Street, Aston.

I did, however, have another, less reputable local cinema. It was really a small flea pit, called the Globe, down the hill from me and opposite the grand old pub, the Barton Arms, and long since demolished. It rarely ran first release films and, accordingly, visiting it was really beneath me. But you could catch an occasional worthy Hollywood B picture there – such as the grey-haired William Boyd's Hopalong Cassidy series. It was there that I had my only brush with paedophilia.

I was sitting alone in the ninepenny seats, inevitably watching a western, *Western Union* (Randolph Scott and Robert Young, since you ask), when an old man arrived to sit next to me. Looking up at the screen, he said, 'That's a lot of buffaloes up there, son.'

'Yes,' I replied.

'A heck of a lot.' Then, still looking at the screen, he undid my trouser buttons and began fondling my penis. I found this a bit disconcerting but I didn't like to offend the old chap, so I stayed where I was for a while. Then I felt it all a bit embarrassing, so I said, 'I'm sorry, but I have to go now.'

He nodded. I said, 'excuse me' and shuffled past him, walked to the back of the cinema, found an empty seat and continued watching the film. I felt neither used nor abused, just a touch annoyed that my concentration had been detracted for a minute or two from the plot.

That's as near as I have got to being harmed by visiting the cinema, and that was nothing. For the rest of the time, it's been a delightful credit balance – and I do so still miss Betty Grable.

Chapter 7

"A MIGHTY LIGHTHOUSE
OF KNOWLEDGE"

T he public library in Albert Road, Aston, looked – and still does – gloomy and forbidding, very much a relic of Victorian civic consciousness: red bricked and blackened by a hundred and twenty years of passing traffic, with iron gates at its foyer folded back, but the whole completely redolent of the original spirit of 1880's idealism. If it is unprepossessing to the modern eye, a more perceptive viewer can pick up the solid *worthiness* of the place. It seems to say: come inside and IMPROVE YOURSELF.

Built in 1880, it was in fact the headquarters of the local civic authority, the Council House, when Aston was independent of Birmingham. At its back now, in a dip forming a car park, are two black doors that used to house the engines and fire pumps of Aston's Fire Brigade. The building became a dedicated public library in 1911, when Aston was merged into the burgeoning Birmingham authority, although a small library existed within it before the takeover. To me, during the war however, it was a treasure trove, at first subservient to and then surpassing those other places of magic, my local cinemas.

I can't remember when I learned to read. I know that it was before I went to my first school, Albert Road Infants, (now rather pleasingly called Prince Albert's Junior/Infant School) at the age of five. I vaguely remember painstakingly picking my way through a review of a Freddie Bartholomew film in a magazine bought by my sister and then, with more fluency, tackling a simple history (more like hagiography) of the life of Nelson, which my father was reading. This precocity impressed my parents and I was immediately taken to the library. In a metaphorical sense, I have stayed there ever since.

Our house was not a temple of literature but it was a place of books. I have referred to Dad's political reading, his self-improvement books and his delight in

Agatha Christie and Mum's addiction to Ethel M. Dell. So we read, all of us. True, there was no place for Henry James or the blessed Jane, but we happily devoured the rubbish of the day. We also listened to the wireless and, although unusually for the time, we disliked the snap and crackle of the ITMA catch phrases, we all gathered around the set for the Askey and Murdoch *Band Waggon* shows and the *Paul Temple* thrillers. My own constant reading, however, was never discouraged and I was never, for instant, rebuked for bringing a book to the table to read at meals – unlike today!

All of those books were borrowed from the public library in Albert Road, for my parents would never think of buying a novel or a work of non-fiction – Dad's self-help tomes were the exception. But my father always felt that reading was vital self-improvement. If you couldn't go to an expensive public school, then at least you could take advantage of the golden treasury on offer at the local library. His feelings, of course, mirrored the Samuel Styles mantra of self help that was a constant theme of the Victorians and was a trickle down from the thrust and vitality of Joe Chamberlain and his fellow civic radicals in their work to improve local amenities in big cities like Birmingham.

The Public Libraries Act was passed in 1850. It permitted councils of towns with populations of ten thousand or more to provide a building, librarian, light and fuel for the lending of books. The aim was that these institutions would serve as both 'workshops of scientific enquiry' but also 'citadels of cultural elevation.' Their immediate growth throughout the country after the Act was passed (Birmingham set about providing libraries in 1860), led to suspicion that they would harbour 'working class political aims.'

This latent right wing Ludditism existed just below the surface of local political life for years and erupted during the years of the depression in the thirties when great pressure was brought to bear on local authorities to cut library services. This was strongly opposed – on the whole, successfully – by librarians throughout the country. In 1937, one librarian wrote to the Liverpool Echo to reveal that slum dwellers visited her library to withdraw popular fiction and that such books:

'transported the reader from the grim realities of life to realms of happiness. Just as opium was a drug for the smoker, so books were a drug for the slum dwellers and would carry them into a state of forgetfulness.'

An opiate for the masses? Hardly that, I would have thought, but it is certainly true that the war brought a modest boom in the use of public libraries. This was despite – or, even perhaps, because of – the damage caused to public bookshelves by the Luftwaffe. After the raid on Coventry, for instance, it was reported that the central library there and many branch libraries had been razed to the ground and some 100,000 books lost. At the war's end it was revealed that fifty public libraries had been destroyed or seriously damaged between 1939 and 1945 and about 750,000 books lost to enemy action. Hitler, the great book burner, had been grimly effective.

As early in the war as 1940, however, the national research agency Mass Observation reported a large increase in the use of public libraries. 'Most libraries,' it stated, 'particularly the better class sort, report a shortening of the time people retain a book and a large increase in the number of books taken out.' This was attributed to the imposition of the black out and the consequent difficulties of going out after dark; the fact that children, deprived of playing in the darkened streets, turned to reading instead; and that the wives of servicemen were finding in literature an antidote to loneliness.

I have no idea if Aston Library was regarded as one 'of the better sort,' but there seems no doubt that it was a busy, even bustling place – in the most somnolent sense, of course – in the early days of the war. Today, for instance, the library stocks just over 26,000 volumes. In 1939, however, there were more than 32,000 books on the shelves, with some 6,500 registered borrowers.

As part of the research for this book, I rang the Head Librarian at my old library, Ms Inge Thornton – she is formally titled Community Librarian now – who, in the middle of a busy day, eased away from her computer screen and talked about her charge. She dug out statistics for me and invited me to visit. I did so.

It is always a huge, if infrequent, pleasure to go back to a place that you once knew well and find that it had changed less than you expected. This was true of Aston Library – well, up to a point. The gloomy but worthy exterior remains unchanged and the strange wooden kiosk inside the entrance, with its long since defunct bell push and sign saying "Enquiries," brought back memories. So, too, did the rather elegant staircase, leading on to the first floor (now let out to offices) where hang heavily mounted grey photographs of former municipal worthies of the once independent Aston local authority. To the left of the entry doors, as ever, is the entrance to the library. All that unchanged.

The library itself, however, is not as I remembered it. Gone are the gloom and the towering adult bookshelves, set close together to form aisles as narrow as tramlines, with all the books bound in cloth as colourless as Newtown Row on a rainy January day. Instead, all is colour and light, with the sun streaming in through the old windows that are now uncluttered to reveal that they stretch almost from floor to ceiling. The space between the shelves now seems to be as broad as Tesco aisles and computer screens for reference are stationed comfortably throughout. Half the books on display are paperbacks, with the rest cased in dust jackets as bright as a Pollock painting. The library now stocks books in nine languages, prominently featuring Bengali and Urdu, but with Somali and Albanian shortly to be added to the list.

The library now adopts a less passive role than when I frequented it. It consistently takes part in ambitious outreach programmes with local schools to encourage youngsters

Leonard Wilcox, the author's father and the youngest of the seven brothers who went to war.

Alfred Wilcox VC, convalescing from a bullet through the ankle in 1918, shortly after winning his medal. The lady on the left is his doctor. Alfred could pull the girls, even when wounded.

I

Ernest Wilcox, DCM, the "cheeky chappy." A temporary Regimental Sergeant Major at 19,
"because there was no one else left!"

Bernard Wilcox MM. He was to lose an eye on the western front.

Alfred's Wedding in 1913. The hero's bride, Louise, is sitting on his left; brother Ernest is standing, top hat in hand, on the far left; brother Leonard is third from left in the middle row; and brother Bernard is holding his daughter, second from right in the back row.

Left: The author as a young reporter in the news room of the Birmingham Gazette, 1954.
Right: The two comrades on Baden Hickman's (Left) wedding day in Manchester, 1965.

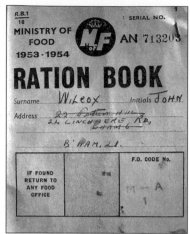

Left: The Headmaster of Aston Commercial School, "the great and the good" Dr W.A. Flack, on the day of his retirement in 1955. Right: The author's war time ration book: one egg and only eight ounces of sugar a week — and NO CHOCOLATE!

Barrage balloons in the sky. What good did they do?

Bomb damage in Birmingham.

Betty Grable. The Pin-up for millions of US troops during the war. We had Vera Lynn.

Aston Public Library. The grim exterior seemed to urge: Come inside and improve yourself!

Aston Commercial School (now Aston Campus. Broadway School.) "It saved my young life."

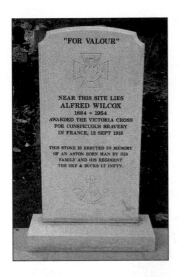

Left: The Memorial to Alfred Wilcox VC, unveiled in the churchyard of Aston Parish Church on 12th September 2006. It removed the tag of Alf as "Birmingham's forgotten VC." Right: The memorial is dedicated.

Elaine Read, Alfred's granddaughter, who found her "lost" family when the VC was sold.

Paul Wilcox on a beach in Portugal in 1978. It was his last holiday. He died seven months later.

Paul's ashes were left at the crematorium in Kent, so the family had no physical reminder of him, until this stone was cut and established in the author's Wiltshire garden in Christmas 2008.

to open a book as well as flick on a mobile phone and, on my visit, it was girding its loins to participate in "The Birmingham Book Bash," the Birmingham libraries' book festival for children and young people.

The number of staff at Aston, however, seems to have remained at roughly the same level as during the war years. Now Ms Thornton has a total of four and half people, which is more-or-less how I remember it, although my recollection of those days is rather coloured by the still vivid memory of a lady whose bosoms were so large that it seemed to my eager gaze she had difficulty in stamping my books. The excitement was heightened for me by the fact that she always seemed to wear a blue angora sweater; a memory indicative, perhaps, of the fact that things weren't quite so colourless during the war as we all like to think.

One unwelcome difference in terms of personnel, however, is that Aston now has a resident security guard, who is on duty every afternoon during the week and all day on Saturdays. 'Just a little fuss with teenagers, occasionally,' says Ms Thornton, 'nothing serious. But we have to take precautions.' The main problem remains what it has always been: pilfering.

Hearing this, I am sure I coloured. I never stole a book, of course, but I was always guilty of smuggling out extra books – those beyond the limit of the two fiction and three non-fiction that we were allowed. Despite the fact that the time given to keep the books was only two weeks (it is four weeks now, with a limit of eight books), there was always one or two works that I felt I just *had* to read, so I would hide them under my pullover and jacket to take them home, unstamped. They were always returned, but I am amazed now at the risk I took, because, if caught, I could never prove, of course, that I was not stealing the things.

Just as I was not a criminal, so too was I not quite the swotty bibliophile that might be presumed from all of the above. Oh, I loved books all right and I would even smuggle an electric torch when I went to bed, so that I could continue to read under the bedclothes long after lights out. (I have to thank my present puffy eyelids for those indiscretions of long ago.) But I was not precocious in my reading choice in those early years.

I began by picking my way along the brightly let children's section in the library, lapping up Richmal Crompton's *William* books but quickly tasting and then rejecting the early children's classics. I found *Alice in Wonderland* silly and literally incredible (and still do) and Enid Blyton's work babyish and condescending. I found myself more at home in the adventurous stuff. The works of Percy F. Westerman were absorbed as were the books of that early Victorian writer Captain Frederick Marryat (*Children of the New Forest; Mr Midshipman Easy* etc). I dismissed Captain Johns' *Biggles* series as soon as he left the First World War but I happily accompanied A.G. Henty to Kabul, the Netherlands, the Pampas, India and Trafalgar and, of course, I sailed with Jim Hawkins and Long John to the Caribbean. Somehow, I missed

Kipling's *Just So Stories* but devoured *The Light that Failed,* although the latter was not strictly a children's book.

In fact, I had soon filleted the rows of children's works and, at about the age of eight at the beginning of the war, I began prospecting into the fascinating, high stacked gloom where the books for adults were kept. I remember doing so nervously at first, because I felt that this must surely be out of bounds for lads like me with short trousers and dirty knees. But not even the magnificently disproportioned lady in the angora sweater said a word, so I set about plundering what became my second home for the next ten years.

At first, I hunted, shifty eyed, for the 'dirty books' I had half heard about. *No Orchids for Miss Blandish,* a terrible disappointment for the prurient, is the only one to remain in my memory, for I was soon onto more fertile and satisfying ground. I sailed with Hornblower against the French and lay behind the rock with *Brown on Resolution;* I helped *Raffles* steal jewels in the great country houses of England and chuckled (rather than belly laughed) at Jeeves and Wooster. But, perhaps most pleasing of all, I discovered Walter Scott and J. Fenimore Cooper.

Scott's medieval romances immediately transported me away from the streets of Aston and the worries about Dad and the war. I learned about and was vastly impressed by the codes of chivalry and morality expounded in such books as *Ivanhoe* and *Kenilworth* and even vowed to live by them myself. This worked quite well until the next mathematics exam came along and I was forced, once again, to cheat (writing tables and formulae on the palm of my hand) to avoid humiliation. As I plodded along the high shelves in the library, however, I found the works of Fenimore Cooper even more impressive.

I dipped into *The Last of the Mohicans* again the other day to remind myself of how well Cooper wrote. I found the text so dense and the style so ornate, however, that I had to give up. The fact that a boy of ten or so was so drawn into these stories says everything about Cooper's ability to create a plot line and pluck at an embryonic imagination so that the boy was transported immediately into the forests of the New World, among the Iroquois and the deerskinned settlers. His eye for detail particularly impressed and remained with me for years. For instance, Hawkeye, the hero of *Mohicans,* always tried to emulate the flat footed walk of the Indians as he trod shod in his moccasins on the trails through the forests, for the distinctive heel and toe impression of the white man left on the carpet of leaves would alert the Indians that an enemy was present. Hawkeye would remember this discipline for miles until, in one moment of mental aberration, the old, natural, way of walking would intrude and he would betray his presence. I loved this nugget of information and, when I came, then, decades later, to write my section on the longwoodsmen of the American War of Independence in my first book, *Masters of Battle,* I stole this detail to give verisimilitude to my story. I tried to check it, but not too vigorously. If it was good enough for J. Fenimore, then it was good enough for me.

I suppose that it could be said that the works of Scott and Cooper (and I learned only the other day that they became great friends – I found that pleasing) were fundamentally boys' stories anyway. If that is so, then they certainly formed for me a bridge to adult works such as those of Conrad and, in contrast, Jerome K. Jerome. Dickens, alas, daunted me and still does and I guess as a boy I needed the lure of adventure or the ability to bring a smile to capture my loyalties. Certainly, Rider Haggard and Anthony Hope enlivened the war years for me and nicely complemented the on-screen heroics of Flynn and Basil Rathbone.

It was later, once I was competing in a workplace with younger people who had all been to university, that I realised how inadequate my literary education had been and – with the help of a dear friend – I set about attempting to read all the so off-putting quality 'stodge' that I had avoided as those years ago. I discovered then that Jane Austen wrote for the world as well as just for women. I found Tolstoy to be probably the most articulate and vivid relater of grand fictional themes the world has known and I wallowed in Flaubert's skill in depicting the hell that women and men can make of a relationship. I struggled a bit with George Eliot, marvelled at James Joyce without understanding his secret, but, on the whole, mastered The Master, Henry James, was annoyed with Virginia Woolf but loved Emily Brontë (although not Charlotte), before launching myself off into the worlds of other giants of the late eighteenth century such as Dostoevsky, Turgenev, Mann, Trollope, and de Maupassant. I realised what I had missed and I learned so much from them all. This late entry into the greats still did not make me well read – I guess I had entered just a touch too late – but it balanced a little what had gone before and lifted my sights.

Now, I cherish the feeling that we may be lucky today to be living in a period as great for writing as was, say, the last quarter of the nineteenth century. I enjoy so much the work of contemporary writers such as Rushdie, Boyd, Barnes, the younger Amis, Byatt, Ishiguro, McEwan, Faulks, Updike, Wolfe, Vidal and Garcia Marques. Only time will tell whether they will stand comparison with the masters of the Victorian era. I hope so.

As a writer myself, I am not fit, of course, to brush the hem of their mosquito nets. I am just grateful that, late in life, I was able to put a foot on the lower rungs of their ladder and to create novels which, amazingly, some people buy and read. For that, I owe everything to that rather forbidding building at the corner of Witton Road and Albert Road in grimy old Aston.

Far more important voices than mine have sung the praises of the public library. Opening a new library in the South of England just after the war, the distinguished economic historian and philosopher Richard Tawney called each one of them "a mighty lighthouse of knowledge."

If by some miracle I should ever justify a blue plaque, I would wish it to be put up outside Aston Public Library with the inscription, "John Wilcox Discovered Books Here."

And that was going to be the end of this chapter until, on opening *The Times* this morning, I read the attached piece by Richard Morrison, a writer on the arts:

"What a great wheeze – to present every 11-year-old in England with a free book by next Christmas. The initiative comes from the educational charity Booktrust. Kids will be able to choose from a list of twelve approved titles. I see – but I daresay that 11-year-olds can get all that from the telly.

"But here's an even better idea. Why not revive something that we used to have when I was a child? I dimly recall that there were these lovely tranquil buildings in every town that contained nothing except thousands of books, and that people of all ages were allowed to borrow these books for nothing or just study and browse in peace. What were they called? Oh yes, I remember – libraries! Whatever happened to them?"

I rest my – and his – case.

Chapter 8

RELATIONSHIPS:
"THE FRIENDLY INVASION"

T he war, of course, didn't change everything. But it altered many facets of British
life – particularly in terms of the way we related to strangers, neighbours,
colleagues and loved ones. The films that came from Carol Reed, Noel Coward
and Gracie Fields, before and during the war, showing bright-eyed, friendly Cockneys
and/or northern mill workers living in each other's pockets had never been truly
representative of the British. On the whole we were a reserved people, anxious to
preserve our individual privacy behind our privet hedges. We had to be. Our islands
were and are small and crowded. As a result, we built barriers to retain a degree of
seclusion and so preserve our sanity.

Two world wars, however, chipped away at those barriers. It was just not possible
to take your sense of privacy with you onto the tube platforms to sleep side by side
with strangers during the blitz, or as you stood in queues every week in the hope of
picking up "something off the ration." The dreadful casualty lists of both wars brought
neighbours together in sympathy and mutual help. Reserved middle class ladies in the
shires learned urban slang from the evacuees billeted on them and young girls who
would normally have gone into genteel occupations in offices and shops now learned
to swear and smoke as they worked in jovial comradeship on munition lines.

The more formal bounds and bonds of family were loosened, sometimes
painfully, by war-time absence. Divorce, normally an indulgence only of the middle
classes and the rich became more widespread as the Dear John letters went out to the
Western Desert, Burma and, later, Normandy. The fortress nature of Britain from
1940 to 1944 had brought in an influx of fighting men from Poland, Czechoslovakia,
Norway, Denmark, Holland, France, Canada, Australia, and, most disturbingly,
America, to present a wider and more exotic choice to British womenfolk. All bets,

it seemed, were off. Fings weren't wot they used to be – and, by the look of it, would never be again.

Entering early teens in Birmingham, I was only faintly aware of these changes. I was much too preoccupied by the daily tragedies of my life: was I about to set up a personal record by coming bottom of the maths exams for the fourth time in succession? Would what I was shamefacedly starting to do really result in blindness? Would Betty Grable be so unthinkingly cruel as to marry John Payne? Then a shadow of the changes occurring in the outside world flickered across my own life in the shape of Edith Harris.

This is not her real name, for she may have relatives still alive in the UK who would not welcome her inclusion in these ramblings. She was the best friend of my sister. They had been together as schoolgirls and stayed close as they had grown up as teenagers and then emerged into their twenties. In some ways, it was a strange alliance in that my sister Margaret was quiet, rather introverted and, although not plain, not obviously good looking. Edith, on the other hand, was opinionated, gregarious and darkly pretty. She lived nearby in Tower Road with her timid mother, a "difficult" epileptic younger brother and a steel worker father who, it was rumoured, often raised his hand to his wife. But not ever, it was said, would he think of hitting Edith. She was too strong.

Edith was a determined and resourceful girl. As the bombing raids increased she decided that whatever happened to the house and to her, she would not survive without decent clothes. So she packed three suitcases with her prettiest dresses and coats and asked her brother to carry them down to the shelter every night. He refused, so she staggered with them herself, never once varying the ritual. Those dresses were needed because her favourite pastime was dancing – and she was good at it. She went out regularly (with a group of girls who excluded my sister) and quickly evolved from the quick step into the jive. Her home was drab, dirty and dispiriting and she spent as little time there as she could, escaping to the dance halls and (with Margaret) to the cinema. She also, however, found a haven – a second home – in our house, where she developed a warm and rather unlikely friendship with my father, in whom she confided the details of her active and sometimes rather chaotic love life. He was, I guess, the sympathetic, amusing and wise patriarch she did not find at home. As for me, I was treated by her with amused tolerance, as the scruffy younger (much younger, for there were seven years between Margaret and me) brother of her best friend and I watched her comings and goings with a mixture of desire and terror.

It was inevitable that Edith, with her good looks, obvious sexuality and longing to escape from her back street home, should marry early. Still in her teens, she became engaged to Ken, a wavy haired young man, very little older than herself, who lived two streets away. It seemed a conventional and almost inevitable match, one destined to follow the ordinary path laid out for working class youngsters in Aston at the time:

courtship, engagement, marriage, children, middle age and, if you were lucky, a dull twilight of old age – all probably played out within a square mile rectangle of the houses in which they had been born.

But things turned out rather differently for Edith.

For some reason, Ken had not joined the forces in the early years of the war. I cannot remember why, because he seemed a healthy young man, good looking too in a conventional way. Perhaps he was in a reserved occupation or possibly had some illness which did not obviously manifest itself. Whatever the reason, Ken never donned uniform. He and Edith, however, did decide to marry and the long process of saving cash and coupons for the happy day was well advanced when the bomb fell on Ken's home in Victoria Road, Aston, in the autumn of 1940. It shattered his leg and he lost what was left of it under the surgeon's knife.

Edith later told my father that the affair had not been going smoothly even before the tragedy – it would have taken a man of unusual attraction and sociological skills to have held her – and that she had decided to end the engagement two days before the bomb fell. In the event, however, she felt that she could not walk out on her fiancé after the blow to him and the two were married as soon as Ken had been fitted with his artificial leg. My sister, of course, was chief bridesmaid.

I am not sure how long they stayed together but I think it was only months before Edith became restive: confined in their rented rooms, pinned down like some exotic butterfly with a man who could not dance and whose spirit could not match hers in its independence and ambition. "I say that she has made her bed and she should lie on it," I remember Ken saying to my father on one of his visits. Trying to do my homework in the crowded living room (our best room, "the front room," was only used on Sundays and at Christmas) was not easy at this time, with Dad being used as a confidante by both sides, but I tried to make myself as inconspicuous as possible as this story of marital breakdown was unfolded. I was damned if I was going to be banished to the cold front room and miss all the fun, although I could not understand why Edith was supposed to lie on her bed all day.

Eventually, of course, they parted and Edith returned to her dark family house and to her old ways: dancing and generally having fun. She became the first person known to our family to file for and obtain a divorce (even Uncle Alf had had to be content with a formal separation).

Set out coldly now, her behaviour seems selfish and even cruel. Yet there was a basic honesty and determination to better herself about Edith that earned admiration from those who really knew her. Her disposition was open and she had a warmth and generosity that it would have been a crime to have confined to two rooms with a man whom she had never really loved. So it was that she earned grudging admiration from neighbours and acquaintances for her independence – even from those old crones who called her a flibbertigibbet.

Yet that hard won respect was soon dissipated by Edith's next act.

By 1943, the prospects for unattached women in the UK had changed since first Edith and Ken had become engaged. The hundreds of refugee servicemen from Europe and the volunteers from the Empire who had gathered in and later passed through Britain as she stood alone against the Axis powers in the early part of the war had then only a peripheral effect on the indigenous population. The incomers had been mainly been confined to harbours on the coastline and the big airfields out in the countryside. It was rather different when the invasion of Europe began its long build up and American soldiers and Air Force personnel began to arrive in Fortress Britain in huge numbers. In September 1943, 76,000 landed and another 175,000 arrived during the following month alone. More than one million were crammed into the UK by the eve of D. Day. General Eisenhower referred to it as the "friendly invasion." Others were not so sure about the accuracy of the adjective.

The point was that the shared language and the ethnic roots of the two countries had became considerable attenuated by 1943. Robert Benchley, New Yorker writer and wit, had famously remarked, "We call England 'The Mother Country' because most of us come from Poland or Italy." And he was right. By the early and mid forties only about one fifth of the US population was of entirely British stock. Approximately five million people had emigrated to the US from the UK during the decades of great traffic in people across the Atlantic, but this was only the third largest contingent after Germany and Italy. During the nineteenth and early twentieth centuries America was third choice for British emigrants, after Canada and Australia. So, when the "friendly invasion" began, England was not the original homeland to thousands of the GIs who landed here. It was just another foreign country, with a language that sounded familiar but was often impenetrable and with manners, traditions and prejudices that seemed not only quaint but often downright antagonistic.

The American authorities realised this and produced a series of guides for their forces stationed in England during the war. If sometimes risible, they were usually full of commonsensical advice and even the occasional compliment to the British, viz:

"British are reserved, not unfriendly. On a small crowded island each man learns to guard his privacy. Don't be misled by the British tendency to be soft-spoken and polite. If they need to be, they can be plenty tough. The English language didn't spread across the oceans and over the mountains and jungles and swamps because these people were panty waists…"

And: "The British don't know how to make a good cup of coffee. You don't know how to make a good cup of tea. It's an even swap."

But the two races soon began to rub up against each other discordantly. The British conservatism and the importance given to tradition irked. "It's stagnation mentality," recorded one American. "If it was good enough for Edward the Confessor it's good enough for us."

Another commented, "Any kind of change was criticised to hell. The landlords and the 'upper crust' looked down their noses at everybody else, including the lowly Yanks. You can call this tradition if you like, but it's more like ignorance and arrogance."

That criticism could probably still be levelled today but, back in 1943–44, the impact of the clash between the two cultures was exacerbated by the sheer size of the invasion and by the differences in standards of living. Henry James, a lover of England, wrote: "It's a complex fate, being American and one of the responsibilities it entails is fighting against a superstitious evaluation of Europe." That sort of arcane epithet might have been suitable for the problems facing rich Americans on the Grand Tour of the Continent in the early 1900s, but it was the comparative wealth of the GIs landing in the UK in the 1940s to fight a different sort of battle that presented problems now.

As early as 1942, the income gap between American and British troops had become noticeable. A private in the British army, for instance, received fourteen shillings a week, while his counterpart in the American forces was paid $13.85 (then equivalent to £3 8s 9d – more than 68 shillings). Questions were raised in the House of Commons and it was not long before the now famous phrase referring to American troops in Britain was on everyone's lips: "Overpaid, over-sexed and over here."

Which brings us back to Edith. Divorce proceedings took time in those days and in 1943, when the GIs first became a presence in Birmingham, she was still technically a married woman. She was no longer a virgin, of course, but she was not promiscuous. Edith, true to herself and with a developed sense of self-worth, did not sleep around. What she did do, though, was dance and when the American camps outside the city began organising dance evenings she was delighted to make up a party with her friends and go along.

It was at such an evening that she met Richard. He was a tall, dark haired, slim and bespectacled doughboy from Maryland, of Jewish parents who had emigrated to the States from Hungary shortly after the First World War. Richard, far from home and of a romantic disposition, immediately fell in love with this pretty brunette who stood no nonsense. They had just two dates together before he was posted away to the South of England for training for the great invasion. They wrote, of course, and Richard asked Edith to marry him and go to the States as soon as the war was over. She, in no way in love with him but tempted by another – and perhaps her last – chance to escape the miseries of back street Aston, asked for time to think about it. She did so for two more years, while Richard slogged his way through Normandy and across to the Rhine.

Despite being in continual action, the boy escaped wounding and stayed true to Edith, always writing, always telling her of the delights of Maryland: good southern weather, parties on the beach at Chesapeake Bay, beers on the deck at the back of his parents' house in Baltimore… Despite the photograph of Richard by her bedside, looking broodingly Bogartian with the collar of his greatcoat turned up, Edith could not recall how he really looked or spoke and, indeed, after only two meetings, what sort of man he was, because, although they wrote often, neither of them was exactly literate. Cruelly, despite making efforts to visit Birmingham as the war in Europe neared its end, Richard was posted straight home and so had no opportunity to press Edith at first hand. Nevertheless, although the letters now came from the States, they remained consistent in content: Edith must come to the States where they would marry and live happily ever after.

It was all too much for the pretty girl from Tower Road. She agreed – on condition that she could come and stay with Richard and his family for a while "to see whether she would like America." This was nonsense. *Of course she would like America.* She knew she would. She had seen enough films to thrill at the thought of the sunshine, the hairstyles, the rich food and the nylons for God's sake! It was really a question of whether she could learn to love Richard and his strange Hungarian family. It was a gamble.

"What if you don't like any of 'em?" I asked her one evening in Potters Hill a couple of weeks before she was due to sail with a shipload of other prospective and actual GI brides. I was now fourteen years old and Edith and I had become chums. She was the only one who didn't smile when I embarked on a Charles Atlas course of body development to turn pimples into muscles. She knew all about self improvement, did Edith.

She shrugged her shoulders. "Then I shall push off to some other part of the States and get a job," she said. "Probably in California."

I was shocked and Margaret, behind Edith, waved to me to pipe down. "But that would be cheating," I said. "You would have gone out there on other people's money under false pretences."

"So what?"

I then delivered a lecture on the morality of evading the principles of the US Government's War Brides Act of 1945. It was a diatribe that faltered before it got into its stride, because its deliverer, consumed by guilt himself on the question of self-abuse and cheating at maths, lost conviction. But Edith didn't mind. She just smiled and gave me a lipsticky kiss.

She left two weeks later at the age of twenty one, embarking on her great adventure and destined to swell the total of 70,000 British women who emigrated to the States as GI fiancées or brides. Other statistics about this great emigration are imprecise and difficult to pin down but it seems to be generally agreed that the majority were young (an average age of twenty three on arrival in the States), had completed schooling to the age of fourteen and came from working or lower-middle-class families. Unlike so many other emigrants, they did not settle into ethnic enclaves but were distributed more or less randomly into American society. They reached the Promised Land, in fact, and then more-or-less dropped out of sight, posing no cultural, religious or political problems.

Edith left behind her two elderly parents that she was destined never to see again, many broken hearts and her best friend, my sister, who missed her greatly. I didn't feel too happy, either.

The American invasion, which had finally swept Edith away, only seemed to lap at Birmingham's outer shores. Most of the American bases were in the south of England or around the airfields of the east and I don't remember ever seeing a GI in Aston. But some of the invaders were to be observed in the heart of the city, loping along Corporation and New Streets, looking languid in their finely tailored khaki green worsted jackets and slacks – so unlike the ugly battledress of British troops – and always, always, chewing gum.

Chewing gum, in fact, became almost a new currency for the Americans. They swapped it for conversation and, it was rumoured, other favours. It was included in the troops' rations and consumption increased six-fold on pre-war levels. In fact, 160 billion sticks of gum were shipped to US forces serving overseas between 1941 and the end of hostilities in 1945. British schoolboys certainly contributed to that consumption. "Got any gum, chum?" became the greeting from the kids as they swarmed around the jaw-chomping visitors and the GIs were undoubtedly liberal in its distribution.

I saw just enough of the American servicemen to be impressed by their seeming nonchalance, the smart cut of their uniforms and the flash of their teeth when they smiled. To me, they all seemed to look like Van Johnson in *A Guy Named Joe*. But I didn't tout for gum and I never actually talked to any GIs. The same was true of my sister – probably because she didn't dance. But, like Edith and millions of other young women of her age, the war changed her life, too.

In 1940, at the age of seventeen, she was immediately conscripted from her office job and transferred to the production line at Hercules, the former cycle factory in Aston, to work on stator winding for armatures, used in aircraft engines. Far from being dismayed at the change, she delighted in it, wallowing in the camaraderie of the other girls on the night shifts and making friends that endured for the rest of her life. But relationships were not easy in this strange, war-torn society. She had one boyfriend but that lasted but a short time – as short as his life as a rear gunner on a Lancaster bomber.

Less innocent was her brief relationship with the departmental manager in her factory, who, a married man and twenty years older, seduced and promised to marry her. It ended in tears, of course, and affected my sister's life adversely through the years when she should have been experiencing other loves. It was not until she was forty that she finally found happiness and married.

And Edith? She married Richard, of course, but it was touch and go for a time. Her life living with his parents was not easy, for they spoke Hungarian around the house for most of the day and Edith felt unwanted and, indeed, intrusive. But Richard stayed true and she learned to love him and rejoice in the higher standard of living she experienced in Baltimore. Her husband learned to fly and would take Edith out for a spin over Chesapeake Bay at the weekends and they eventually had a son, Richard Junior. Once the boy began his schooling, Edith took a job as a bank teller and year by year slipped more and more into the American way of life.

Yet she never forgot Aston and her friends there. She returned quite early after her departure to bury her mother – her father had long since died – and we saw, even then, a slightly plumper and less abrasive Edith. She visited twice in later years with Richard and my sister made reciprocal visits to Baltimore. On one of them, Edith confided that she still yearned for England and might return for good one day, but no-one really believed her, for she had become satisfied with most things American. It was, then, a happy ending to Edith's search for freedom and a fuller, richer, way of life. Alas, she died eleven years ago from cancer but feeling fulfilled, she said, to the end. Richard married again and, now in his eighties, remains a firm friend of my family.

I have no idea if Edith's experience is typical of those caught up in "the friendly invasion." With the exception of her cancer, I just hope so.

Chapter 9

FRIENDSHIP

"I count myself in nothing else so happy,
As in a soul rememb'ring my good friends."
William Shakespeare.

"Grief can take care of itself, but to get the full value of joy,
you must have someone to divide it with."
Mark Twain.

"A man, sir, should keep his friendships in good repair."
Samuel Johnson.

Google "friendship" and the search machine answers with 63,200,00 entries. If there is a more popular heading on the net, then it would be mind bogglingly time consuming to find it – and the quotations listed above are only three of hundreds that snuggle together amicably (well, they would, wouldn't they?) in my reference book under that heading. So we can take it that friendship is one of the most important elements in human relationships. Acquaintances form the essential lubrication of social intercourse and without them we would all become hermetic shells and shrivel. But friendships, the acquaintances that grow and *last,* are the very sinews of life itself and without them we would cease to exist as individuals. So it has been with me, anyway, throughout my life. Where would I have been without Jim, Nigel, Peter, Liam, Tony, Brian, Albert, Mac, Jane, Kathleen, Mary, Glenne and Sharon?

Because this book is restricted to a chronological timeframe, however, the name that has cropped up in the context of friendship most often has been that of Baden Hickman, my closest childhood and teenage friend, in the years immediately before the war, through the war years themselves and immediately afterwards. He therefore demands a part of this book, albeit only of vignette length, all to himself.

We first met at infants' school when we were about six years old and continued as classmates together, although not as particularly close friends, into junior school, until, as related, I moved next door to him in Ettington Road, in 1937. Then we bonded and our paths followed remarkably parallel routes until the mid fifties.

I was the senior by three months and, as a result, was the leader, until, that is, I was unwise enough in the school playground to tell another boy that I could fight Baden. This business of physical domination was important in the hierarchy of the classroom. You did not have to go to the lengths of actual physical combat to assert superiority. Age usually did that, irrespective of size – at least in the early years. Later, these things could be put to the test and that was true that day in the playground. By this time, Baden had become tall for his age (he reached his full height of 6ft 2ins by his mid teens) and he immediately wrestled me to the ground. That was that and he became more-or-less the boss for the next few years, until these things didn't matter any more.

The role fitted him, for he was much more daring than I. It was Baden who climbed up the various drainpipes of Aston Commercial School and inched his way along the apex of the roof, waving to me as I stood about one hundred feet in the playground below, not daring to look up at him, my stomach twisted with vertigo. It was he who suggested one evening, in the early days of the blitz, that we should hide in an old tool shed in our garden – and stay there. We did so and caused anguish to both sets of parents until we finally emerged in the early hours of the morning. And it was Baden who bowled at cricket as fast as the wind and who could kick a football into infinity, or so it seemed.

We were inseparable for a decade, as we went through the same schools. In our later years at the ACS, I inched ahead of him marginally in terms of leadership and won the title of School Captain from him only by a hairsbreadth, according to a member of staff. Yet I was always more dependent on him than he on me. Baden – he was named presumably after Baden Powell, the creator of the Scouts, although he never wore the neckerchief and woggle – always had an inbuilt sense of independence that sometimes made him resistant to the closeness of our relationship. In our early years together I would call on him to come out and play, only to be met by his mother who would smile, shake her head and tell me that he wanted to stay in by himself. "Isn't he a funny boy, John?" she would ask. It didn't seem a rhetorical question, because she seemed puzzled herself by his periods of introspection.

Then the partnership broke up when I went into the army to do my National Service and he, the great athlete, was rejected because he had flat feet. We did, however, enter journalism together. He took the established route of starting on a local weekly, reporting courts, flower shows and parish council meeting. I began, less impressively, as a tea boy in the sub-editors' room of one of Birmingham's two evening newspapers before becoming a junior reporter and, later, feature writer. Inevitably, we began drifting apart, mainly because Baden followed his career to Nottingham and then Manchester, while I stayed in Birmingham before making the big leap to London. Of course, we stayed in touch and shared many things in common – a love of Aston Villa and, *inter alia,* a desire to make a name for ourselves as journalists. When I won an award as "The Young Journalist of the Year" the first letter of congratulation I received was from Baden, now working on the *Manchester Evening News.* But that feeling of brotherliness had slipped away.

Looking back now, I realise that it was not just geographical distance that caused this. By his early twenties, Baden's occasional bouts of introspection had developed into a firm and abiding belief in Christianity. He was by no means an intellectual – he evinced no interest in the theatre or films and hardly ever seemed to read a book other than the Bible or the memoirs of some Fleet Street figure. But he argued passionately in defence of his faith when I attacked it with my agnosticism ("come on, you're a journalist. No emotion, man. The facts. Where are the facts?")

By this time he had developed, it has to be said, a rather pompous air. He exuded gravitas and, later, with his height and now bald pate, he even looked like a bishop. Nevertheless, when I married ridiculously young at 22, Baden, of course, was Best Man. Fourteen years later he returned the compliment and I flew to Manchester for his wedding to Shirley.

She was probably the best thing that ever happened to Baden. A former beauty queen and imposingly tall in her own right, she was a striking red head who used gently to take him down when he became too fustian. They had two sons, both of them dominatingly tall.

Baden's belief, which Shirley shared, had become the most important thing in his life and he became the respected churches' correspondent of *The Guardian*, using his journalistic skills to shed light on all denominations. He also became the friend of bishops but was not afraid to give publicity to church politics, in what the sub editors called "Baden's holy rows." I berated him when he left all this to take his family to the Seychelles to become a journalistic missionary with the Far East Broadcasting Association, beaming Christian propaganda to India and the eastern coast of Africa, and I adopted what must have been an infuriatingly smug "I told you so" attitude when he returned home, in reduced financial circumstances and ill. But he went back again, with similar results.

Then back he came, *en famille,* to Manchester once again and took up a post with the Central Office of Information, carrying out radio work for overseas listeners (that orotund voice, now cleared of its Birmingham accent, was impeccably suitable for this) and escorting royalty on their visits to the north. He was eventually awarded the MBE and Betty and I welcomed him from the other sides of the gates as, with Shirley, he left Buckingham Palace, beaming.

His decline, alas, was quick and tragic in its ending. Baden developed a rare form of Parkinson's disease, which affected his neck and speech, so that his head fell forward and he became voiceless. Shirley looked after him devotedly, of course, but it became too much for her and arrangements were made for him to go into full care nursing. On the day that Baden was due to picked up by the ambulance to go into the nursing home, Shirley went early morning shopping. Cruelly, her bag, containing money and credit cards, was snatched from her in the street. On returning home, upset of course, she picked up the telephone to report to the police and sustained a heart attack and died immediately. Baden, mute and virtually paralysed by now, could only sit, watch and wait for help.

Betty and I visited him in hospital some months later. The paralysis had become worse and affected his face so that it, *and even his eyes,* were completely devoid of expression. It was like looking at an empty house, although he could communicate laboriously by spelling out words by pointing to a board containing letters. We left shortly afterwards, tears pouring down our cheeks, my old friend's blank, staring eyes following us as we walked down the ward. He died a few days later, on 16th March 2000, ten days before his 69th birthday.

In its obituary, *The Guardian* wrote of his Christianity and continued: *"…but he made no great issue of it. Instead, he did good by stealth. If the books editor had review copies to give away, he would bag a suitable collection for the Salvation Army, for prisoners at Strangeways Prison in Manchester, for his local hospice, or to distribute to down and outs under the railway arches…"*

He was a better man than me and I miss him still.

Chapter 10

THE GOOD OR
THE BAD OLD DAYS?

Three distinguished scientists – an expert in internal combustion, a specialist in ballistics and an economist – were marooned on a desert island and they were starving, with no food to eat but a tin of baked beans. They had no means of opening the tin but they put their Great Minds to the task. The internal combustion expert insisted that the solution was to build a fire, put the tin in the flames and the heat would explode the tin. No, said the ballistics man. Throw the tin against a rock and eventually the force of impact would break the tin. The economist thought for a moment and then said: "First, let us presume we have a tin opener…"

No. I agree. Not the funniest beginning to a chapter that you have ever read but it does have a kind of relevance to the question I have been pondering: how would a child psychologist rate the period from age eight to fourteen in terms of its importance in influencing later life? I can't help feeling that the answer would be approached in the same kind of cop out way as that taken by the economist, viz: it all depends on the circumstances.

Well, my circumstances were ordinary and extraordinary, in that, for those crucial years, I was brought up in a conventional and loving home in a country that was a main protagonist in a world war that killed more people than ever before. With the exception of the long illness of my father, my family was not unusual and, indeed, it could be argued that I was raised in a typical working class environment. Except that attempts were made to kill me by aerial bombardment when I was eight and for most of the period I lived on a frugal diet imposed by those circumstances.

So, how was I (and by extension, millions of other children of that age) affected by the experience? It would be wrong to generalise, of course (ah, a touch of that economist creeping in here?), so let me concentrate on the personal and force myself to be self-analytical about the experience and its effects.

In terms of personal loss, my family escaped. No one near and dear was killed or wounded in the fighting. Britain, in fact, got away comparatively lightly in terms of fatalities during the war, losing 326,000 fighting men (compared to 750,000 in World War I) and figuring at number fourteen in the table of losses sustained by nation states. Put alongside the dreadful figures for Russia (8,668,000 killed), Germany (3,250,000) and China (1,324,000), it seems that we fought a war of caution and, befitting a country with small resources of manpower, prudent commitment of our servicemen. Nevertheless, the wounds sustained by my father in 1916 created the illness which hung over our small family until his death in 1945 and made me aware, beyond my years, of the price to be paid when a nation goes to war. Yet the experience did not turn this young liberal into a pacifist. On the contrary, the war imbued me with views about military intervention which have stayed with me until this day.

Once the facts about the Germans' policy of genocide against the Jews and the Japanese treatment of prisoners of war had began to emerge after the end of hostilities, there was no way that my benevolent attitude towards the ordinary citizens of those countries ("they're just like us, really, aren't they?") could be maintained. If only our Government had paid more attention to the *Kristallnacht*, when the Nazis' attitude to the Jews was first revealed... if only we hadn't appeased Hitler... So a young interventionist was born.

It has been a philosophy that has not been easy to adhere to over the years. I had to make rules. For instance, the young Wilcox was strongly against the Suez adventure of 1956 and furious when it became clear that the Government had lied to Parliament. That invasion was clearly prompted by an ill-judged, colonialist desire to hold on to what was perceived to be a national asset that should, in fairness, have been negotiated away to the Egyptians years before. No, in my view, intervention had to be justified by a set of circumstances that would save lives in the end: the removal of a brutal dictator operating without democratic mandate who was a threat to surrounding countries, for instance. And it had to be militarily feasible. So Kosovo was right, Sierra Leone was right – and so, was Iraq, although possibly I am the last man left to believe that.

Yet the pacifists have a case. My good friend Jim has recently come out of the closet and, after much thought, has declared himself a pacifist and as such is against military force of all kinds (he concedes, of course, the need for national police forces which may have to exert regularised force to keep the peace). Apart from his basic precept that it is wrong to take life, his argument runs something like this: it would have been better to have given way to Hitler in 1939 – and Japan earlier in China – and let both countries have their way. This would have saved the 61 million lives that were lost in World War II. But what about the evils of National Socialism in Germany and imperial militarism in Japan? Surely the world would have been a far worse place if they had been allowed to run untrammelled? No, he argues, the greater evil was the appalling loss of life that the war caused ("violence creates violence; pacifism stems that continuity"). These systems would have run their course and would eventually have collapsed in on themselves by nature of their very unsustainable immorality, as did Russian communism.

It's an interesting argument but I believe a false one. Such a policy of laissez faire would surely encourage every little – or large – tin pot dictator to do what he liked, since world opinion and the muscle to back it would not pose a threat to him. And who is to say that the total cost of letting Nazism and Japan militancy run riot over decades without opposition would not have exceeded the 61 million lives that opposing them produced?

But I digress and run ahead of my story. What other effect did the war have on kids like me? Well, the imposed wartime diet did all of us little harm. In fact, as I have recorded, dieticians now claim that those fat-light, fibre-strong (bread wasn't rationed until well after the war was over, remember) meals were good for everyone. Perhaps the damp of those nights in the air raid shelter did breed the rheumatism that impedes me a touch now, but I played cricket regularly until I was 68 so it's doubtful if I can really blame Hitler for denying me full mobility. (Somehow, without knowing it, I seem to have contracted a mild form of polio during the war. When I limped into my doctor's surgery with a cricket injury some twenty years ago, he noticed on examination that the calf on my right leg was one and half inches shorter in circumference than that on my left. Ah, polio, he said, probably contracted from a public swimming bath as a boy. Without it, I would undoubtedly have played cricket, football, tennis and probably tiddlywinks for England, but, again, I doubt if we can blame the war for that.) Perhaps the most lasting influence the war years have had on me, in terms of food, is that our fruit bowl is now never without bananas and the bottom shelf of our freezer bulges with choc ices.

Did the war hasten the onset of the women's lib movement? I doubt it. It is true that the eventual emancipation of women begun by the drafting into factories of female labour in World War I was further supported by the conscription of women in 1940. All able-bodied single women over 21 were sent either into the Land Army, the armed services or factory work in metal and chemical industries, shipbuilding or vehicle manufacture. But heavy lobbying by the powerful trade union movement ensured that, by law, all of those jobs had to be relinquished to returning servicemen after the war. The robust comradeship and sense of independence born on the factory assembly line during the war, must have helped to create a healthier balance to the sexes in post war life, but the gender revolutionaries of the sixties and seventies were not of that generation. Certainly, I never caught my sister attempting to burn her bra.

For people in Britain who did not lose dear ones in the conflict, I suggest that it is not the war years that left the most enduring legacy but the immediate post war period. This was a time of unexpected misery and deprivation. Germany and Japan defeated, the Empire territories regained, a Victory parade – but rationing extended, no coal, the worst winter in 1947 for years, and all our illusions about a Socialist new dawn gradually crushed by our poverty as a nation as the debts to America were called in. We had fought two world wars and emerged as one of the principal victors. Yet we had sacrificed most of our overseas investments to fight the wars and we were broke.

The personal disillusion was real. I remember as a schoolboy feeling pride that this fabulous Empire on which the sun never set had emerged from the war still intact and that I was damned lucky to be born British. As a result, I couldn't understand why everything (apart, of course, from Miss B. Grable) was so very, very grey. There were just no chocolates to be had, anywhere. Who had won the bloody war, then?

Yet, as I emerged into the full misery and joy of my teenage years, I – and, I hope, millions of contemporaries – rose above the gloom.

There was the conventional excitement of growing up to be suffered and enjoyed, as everyone before me had experienced, war or no war. The wonder of what the world could offer – love, success, fulfilment – was on offer, just as it had always been and I felt no different, I guess, from all those teenagers who had tingled with expectation over the decades that had gone before.

Now, as I sit in the Old Fart's corner of the Black Dog, my local in Wiltshire, those days seem to my present contemporaries to be lit by a rosy glow. Those were the days *indeed*. *Not* the bad old times – a handful of grit for breakfast, a cardboard box on the M1 to live in, as described so belly-achingly wittily by the Pythons in that famous sketch from the first Policeman's Ball. No, they said, things were so much better then: a low crime rate, young people behaving themselves, a pint of bitter for 2s 6d, footballers being paid the proper rate for their solitary afternoon's work. No mugging, only Englishmen as your neighbours (oh, all right then, just a few Scotsmen, Welsh and Irish) and local shops that provided good service. The harrumphing that goes on at that end of the bar is so persistent that it almost brings down the plaster.

Yet, despite my age and clear memories of the excitement of my youth, I don't join in. I reject the argument that any yesterday could have been a golden age. On the whole things are better today; in fact they nearly always are, at whatever point you take the comparison.

This argument, of course, opens the floodgates. What about crime? We used to be able to go out and leave our doors unlocked. Not now. What about the cost of housing? Young folk today can't get even a toehold on the housing ladder. And what about violence in the cinema and on the telly? Nothing but beatings, car chases and explosions. And so on.

Of course, the debate is not capable of rational conclusion because the subject matter is so subjective. Crime rates? Statistics are used by both sides to prove opposing points of view. Housing costs? Well, as I write this, they have lurched down in the credit crunch and are creeping up again, but even before that, the incomes of most people seemed to cope with house prices. Violence on the little and large screens? Doesn't anyone remember the brutal Klu Klux Klan scenes in the Birth of a Nation (1915), the lynchings in the Oxbow Incident (1943) or the awful rape in Clockwork Orange (1971)? The new and terrible threat to the people living in our cities posed today by Muslim suicide bombers? Yes, but aren't they in a direct line of descent from the nihilistic terrorists of the early part of the twentieth century, or, indeed, the IRA bombers at the end of it?

So, in forming a view, one searches for some way of leaving subjectivity behind.

I go to those areas where it is possible to be *objective* about the comparisons. Statistics which don't cancel out – such as birth rates in this and other developed countries. The rate of child deaths at birth is much lower than in 1945 and we live longer now, to the point where our longevity is posing problems to the health service and social security systems. Medicine has improved and the old killers like diphtheria, smallpox and tuberculosis are things of the past in countries like the United Kingdom. We can even swap old hearts for new! Dentists no longer extract decayed teeth as they did in my youth. Now they drill them (painlessly – oh the terror of that old slow drill!) and cap them so that kids today have smiles that George Clooney would envy.

In those areas of human activity where statistics are vital, the rate of improvement is precisely defined. We run faster, jump further, throw cabers and javelins over greater distances, swim quicker, leap higher and lift heavier weights than ever before. It is most unusual for an Olympic Games to conclude without one or more world records being broken.

Of course, death and destruction have not been removed from the world and new threats emerge relentlessly. We no sooner find a cure for leprosy and diphtheria than Aids creeps across the globe. We set up highly sophisticated seismic measuring devices across the world and then a tsunami crashes in without warning to show how puny are our efforts. World climate change has suddenly – alarmingly suddenly – emerged to pose what is probably the greatest challenge mankind has yet faced.

Yet, given the resources of the human spirit, I have confidence that these new threats will be overcome. To repeat, where these things can be objectively measured, the facts show that the human race does make progress. On balance, things *are* better than they used to be.

We build on the past and on the successes of others. To end this part of my story where I began, with my uncle Alfred: if he had not been inspired to display such great bravery when "he went mad" in 1918, I would never have become a novelist. It was wondering whether I would ever have had the courage to do what he did, that led me to attempt to examine the nature of courage in my first novel, *The Horns of the Buffalo,* which led in turn to a writing career.

Looking back at my childhood, then, I have no regrets, nor desire to return to those old days. I have warm and sustaining memories of dear parents and good friends; when low, I can always recall a Technicoloured vision of Miss Grable singing (ever so slightly off key) *Put Your Arms Around me Honey, Hold me Tight;* and my post-war home eventually became replete with bananas and choc ices. In terms of childhood memories, then, what more could a chap want?

Part II

THE YEARS IN BETWEEN

Chapter 11

"SILLY LITTLE SOD"

B ut life, of course, is made up of more than merely childhood memories and it
would be unfair on the reader to leave him at the point where a shy and
innumerate boy emerges into a post-war world full of excitement and
promise – not least when the most tragic and in many ways the most compelling
event was waiting to happen.

Not yet, though, not yet. The story must unfold in its own way, as the boy
becomes a man and then, perhaps with the measured step of a Greek tragedy, takes
on the responsibilities of joys and fatherhood.

Baden and I entered the job market together in September 1947. It was not a
good time to be seeking a foothold in journalism. Men and women were still
returning from the Forces, some with distinguished records earned in the fierce
fighting of the last few months of the war and they took priority, of course, in the
jobs' stakes. Journalism was probably the last of the "open" professions, not
demanding a university degree or other professional qualification. But Baden and I
could not even offer the conventional base line of having gained our School
Certificate – roughly equivalent to possessing five of today's O levels – because the
ACS did not teach entry to it. Nevertheless, we had both earned Royal Society of
Arts certificates in English and, more importantly, we could type and write shorthand
at at least 120 words per minute.

Even so, it was a surprise when we secured jobs almost immediately. Baden
became a junior reporter on a small group of weekly newspapers in the Midlands,
covering the conventional round of garden fetes, parish council meetings,
weddings and funerals. My foothold was on an even lower rung of the ladder: as
a subs' boy with the Birmingham Evening Despatch, the second of the two
evening papers in the city. I was paid thirty shillings a week, five shillings more
than Baden earned.

To say the work was undemanding would be gilding the lily. It was the life really of an office boy, albeit in a rather unusual setting. The work place was a large room where some fifteen to twenty sub-editors sat at a large table, working heads down, pencils racing, editing individual stories for the editions as they came and went through the day. Their job was to ensure the accuracy and grammar of the pieces, to cut them to size when necessary, and to add headlines and cross heads to each one. At the centre of the table sat the terrifying figure of the Chief Sub Editor, Cyril Ticquet, presiding like the conductor of some muted orchestra as he hurled copy around the table and shouted inexplicable (to me) instructions to his players about the type face to be applied to each story. Ticquet was an ex-Squadron Leader – former ranks were still important then – with an erect bearing and a Germanic appearance, featuring skull-clipped grey hair and rimless spectacles. To me, he was Attila the Hun and Heinrich Himmler rolled into one. Yet I had cause to be grateful to him later.

We subs' boys ran errands for the subs, fetched endless mugs of tea for them as they worked through the day and brought up from the canteen plates of greasy eggs and chips for lunch. We huddled together in a corner of the room where a group of suction tubes curved down, emitting a low hiss like a group of grey pythons, waiting to pounce. Their prey were the sheets of copy which the individual sub would hold up with a cry of "copy down, boy" when the story was marked up. One of us would then spring forward, grab the story, fold it once and clip it into a short cylinder, then feed it into one of the pythons which would suck it in and, hissing even louder, send it down to the waiting compositors on the floor below.

As the deadlines for each page and each edition neared, the atmosphere in the subs' room was a mixture of intense concentration and speed, then of immediate relaxation as the time was met. Chairs were pushed back, cigarettes lit and conversations begun. Then it all began again. Missing a deadline, of course, was the greatest sin and speed was everything. When a sub shouted "copy down" we jumped to it.

The role of the boys was basic and menial, of course. Yet, as the editions rolled out, I felt that I was part of a great machine, producing this miracle of feeding the one million plus population of Birmingham with news accurately written, brightly presented and bang on time some six (I think) times a day.

However, one day I undoubtedly took the need for speed perhaps a touch too far. I was given an urgent message from one of the subs to take to Mr Ticquet, who, for some reason, had temporarily left his podium at the head of the table. I wandered around the building and eventually pinned him down to the urinal. There, as he stood contemplating eternity as he relieved himself, I presented him with the message. He took it, buttoned his fly and said: "Nothing is this urgent, you silly little sod…"

I was given the job because a vacancy occurred when the senior subs boy, John Leese, was promoted to become a down-table sub on the sports desk of our sister morning paper, The Birmingham Gazette. On my first day, and his last, he took me round to show me the ropes.

He was a lean, tall, gentle lad whom I instinctively liked. As he instructed me about who liked one egg or two and how many sugars the Chief Sub demanded, I wondered how far he would go in his career. In the event, it was quite a way, for he became editor of the Coventry Evening Telegraph and then was making a splendid fist of the editorship of the London Evening Standard, arguably the most important evening paper in the land, when he died tragically and prematurely in, I think, his late forties.

I had lasted about two months as a subs' boy when the great Mr Ticquet noticed one day that I took his luncheon order in shorthand.

"What speed can you do?" he demanded. I muttered something about 120 words a minute, he grunted and that was that. But two weeks later I was promoted to become a copy-taker on the night shift, working for the morning paper, The Gazette.

In fact the shorthand was hardly needed, although it was supposed to be a basic requirement for the job. The work consisted of sitting at a typewriter, earphones clamped to the head, and typing the stories telephoned in by the district reporters operating within a radius of roughly fifty miles around Birmingham. The hours were uncongenial – 2.30 to 10.30 – although I often stayed later on busy news nights. Once my typing was up to speed (I plodded to begin with) the work was not demanding, but it took me closer to news reporting and, as I sat in quieter moments, I could see a corner of the large reporters' room, where my idols worked a shift system, one shift working for the evening paper and the other for the Gazette.

Like the Evening Despatch, the newspaper was owned by a large provincial group, the Westminster Press, which included such famous publications as the Northern Echo and the Oxford Mail. The Gazette was a broadsheet, of course, for the advantages of the tabloid format had not then been established, and it was a brightly written, well produced paper – much more readable, I always felt, than the more staid and famous opposition, the Birmingham Post. Yet the Gazette was the older of the two and, in fact, the second oldest daily newspaper in the UK.

I have today on he walls of my study, carefully preserved between sheets of glass, the edition for Monday 8th November 1742 and containing – on its *front page,* mind – the reassuring news that the Empress of Russia intended to use her good offices, with the Emperor of Prussia, to Restore the general Tranquillity of Europe. Ah yes! We were always wide ranging in our news coverage. In fact, the Gazette, with a circulation of roughly 90,000 copies a day, completely outsold the Post with its 40,000, although the opposition Birmingham Mail had a much larger circulation than the Evening Despatch.

I loved the Gazette, with its virtually unique support for the Liberal Party and well regarded sports coverage. I banged away happily, afternoon and evenings, in the copy-taking room, sometimes on my own, at the expense of my social life. I hardly noticed, in fact, that I had received no increase to my thirty shillings a week since leaving school. It was the great and good – and now not quite so terrifying – Cyril Ticquet who came to my aid once again. He had been installed as editor of the Gazette and immediately increased my wages to two pounds four shillings a week. More importantly, however, he promoted me once again and gave me entry to the wonderful world of news reporting. I was a writer at last!

I had just three months of covering small stories and gradually learning the need for speed, accuracy and originality in writing that news reporting for a daily newspaper demanded. Then, just as my confidence was growing and I was beginning to realise that this was the work that I was born to do, the King called me to take his shilling and, in May 1948, I reported to Aldershot and began my stint as a National Serviceman.

I knew it was coming and, to be honest, I was rather looking forward to it. Much as I loved my new work, I had never left home before and the thought of actually firing a rifle, instead of merely reading about it, intrigued me. With thoughts of my father and those redoubtable uncles still very much in mind, I was happy to be a soldier, at least for the statutory eighteen months. I had never been abroad and, although the war was over, there was still unrest around the world and the British Army was patrolling trouble spots. It could, it just could, be exciting.

But it was not.

At the initial placement interview, it was made perfectly clear that there was no chance of a commission. That was for graduates and ex-public schoolboys. Shorthand? Ah good. You will be a clerk. So into the Royal Army Service Corps I went. It proved to be NOT the army.

After an initial six weeks of basic training – square bashing, rifle cleaning, the shock of sharing a shed full of boys who slept only in their new issue, sandpaper-like army shirts and said f**k in every sentence – I was singled out. It was to be the War Office, not Bermuda, Malaya, Hong Kong nor even Germany, but bloody London. On a very hot day in June, wearing Field Service Marching Order and carrying a kitbag, I trudged around Belgravia looking for the W.O. clerical staff sorting office. There, a kindly sergeant (I didn't know such people existed) gave me a chair and a cup of tea and sent me off to Mrs Hayes in Victoria, asking me to pass on his regards to her.

This lady proved to be as redoubtable in her way as the great Ticquet. Large and with a moustache and cockney accent, she kept a large four storey house near Victoria Station into which, four to a room, were crammed War Office clerks, mainly National Servicemen. She provided breakfast, a large pot of tea in the evening and one small bathroom to be shared by us all.

My work lay in the Department of Manpower Planning in Lansdowne House, Berkeley Square, part of the large empire controlled by the Adjutant General, the virtual second-in-command of the Army. The building had been a large hotel before the war and bathrooms still proliferated but it was really a warren of small rooms. I entered what was really a Civil Service world, where we were allowed to wear civilian clothing and everyone, it seemed, was known by his initials. The Major General who ran the Directorate was known as DMP, his two Brigadier deputies, DDMP(A) and (B), and the Colonels who ran the various departments making up the Directorate were designated CAG10, or whatever. The Major General had a Warrant Officer Grade II as his personal assistant or PA and the two Brigadiers a Staff Sergeant each. They were known respectively as PA/DMP, PA/DDMP(A) and PA/DDMP(B). Got it? Well, I didn't. Not for ages, anyway.

Because I was bright, could draft a letter, showed I could take minutes of meetings, had a good telephone manner and could do shorthand and typing better than anyone else, I was soon made a sergeant and became PA/DDMP(B), even looking after the tiny, dynamic Major General Henry Bainbridge C.B., C.B.E., when his Sergeant Major was away. It was fun – sort of – for a time and I began to enjoy London, particularly in discovering the central parks, "the lungs of London," and cautiously extending the little culture I had acquired in Birmingham. I saw "Les Enfants du Paradis" in a tiny cinema near Victoria Station, revelled in the gentle satire of Flanders and Swann in "At the Drop of a Hat" and was in the gods at Covent Garden when Victoria de Los Angeles made her debut in "Boheme".

But it wasn't journalism. I began to itch to return to my career and counting the days until I would be demobbed. Then disaster struck. The North Koreans poured over the border with South Korea and a prospective World War III stared everyone in the face. It was clear that Britain must send troops to support the Americans who were now propping up the remnants of the South Korean Army and the focus fell on our little General and his department of manpower planning. At about this time I was taking the minutes of a meeting between the General, his two Brigadiers and several Colonels when it suddenly dawned on me: the idiots were going to propose extending the period of national service from eighteen months to two years! Typing up the minutes, it occurred to me that I could perhaps substitute twenty months for twenty four, slip it through and so earn the gratitude of thousands of National Servicemen. But lacking the courage of Uncle Alf I funked it. So my servitude was extended.

With just a couple of months to go, Captain Smith, the diminutive Staff Officer controlling the offices of the Directorate, called me in. Suede-booted, moustached and a with a nose spread all over his face as a result of being kicked by a mule in India, Smithie was a delightful man.

"Look," he said, "Eisenhower is coming back to take command of European armies in an alliance to be called NATO. He is going to be based in France. He wants a top notch office with plenty of Brits in it. I will put you forward if are up for it. You will immediately become a Warrant Officer and a commission will almost certainly follow. It will be a chance to be close to an amazing man. I can't guarantee you'll get it but the General will support you, I know. It will mean signing on, of course. What do you say?"

I said no. It was without hesitation and perhaps I should have thought more deeply. But I still feel the decision was right. Warrant Officer, commissioned or not, it was still the job of a Super Clerk. And I wanted to be a good journalist. Not an office worker.

So my time for departure came at last and I hurried back to 22 Potters Hill, Aston, Birmingham, to mother's cooking and to the reporters' room at the Gazette. There, things had changed. The shift system had ended and the morning paper had its own team of reporters and its own News Editor, Don Horobin. Cyril Ticquet had gone, to edit the Group's weekly paper, the Sunday Mercury, and the Gazette was now edited by a distant, scholarly man named Charles Fenby. I fell into line as the most junior of the reporting team.

The next four years were among the happiest of my working life. They can perhaps best be summed up by the opening lines of a book of Fleet Street reminiscences written by a famed reporter – so famed, alas, that I have forgotten his name. He began his story like this: "Don't wear flannels and a sports jacket to work today, dear," said my wife. "You might have to interview a king." "Rubbish," I said. "That day I interviewed a king…"

I never interviewed a king but the life of variety encapsulated by the anecdote became mine. I covered virtually every different type of story that a good, provincial, daily paper hack could tackle: murders, long, convoluted court cases, bishops' enthronements, the Queen's Coronation as seen from the back streets of Birmingham, train crashes… I did the occasional book review, covered theatrical opening nights and interviewed celebrities ranging from Danny Kaye to Max Bygraves. I ran a gossip column for a while – and even improved my formal education.

This came about because this last of the "open professions" decided that it should create some kind of basic standard for entry to it and for juniors already working as journalists. It therefore set up a training scheme, with an examination at the end of it. It was a nation wide structure, created by several industry bodies, and I underwent a year of studying subjects including economic history, English language and literature, local and national government and elementary law as applied to publications. Shorthand was there, too, but that was a breeze for me, although I extended my speed to 140 words per minute. I attended lessons at Birmingham University, somehow fitting them in with my reporting round and romped through the final examination. There was, you see, no mathematics!

I was told that I had passed – although one or two of my young colleagues did not – but not how well I had done, until it was announced that I had won a prize as the "Young Journalist of the Year," a title and honour I had no idea existed or that I was eligible for. I must have impressed someone!

The prize was the best bit. I had to put forward a journalistic assignment that would take me overseas for a month. It was to be a journey that would be completely my own invention, i.e. not one proposed by my employers, although my editor, I was told, had every right to advise me. The idea would be to write feature type material and send it back to the paper for publication in the Gazette – and, if it was deemed good enough, by other papers in the Westminster Press Group.

The withdrawn Charles Fenby had by now in fact completely withdrawn to London and in his place as editor was a strong, sociable ex-Daily Express man, Maurice Cheesewright. He urged me to go to an unheard of place in Germany called Wolfsburg, where a small motor manufacturer was producing a ridiculously old fashioned looking car named a Volkswagen, which, it was reputed, could one day challenge the models we were producing in the Midlands. Germany? Hell no. I had a better – well, more attractive to me – idea. I announced that I would go to Spain and interview Franco.

Amazingly, no one tried to talk me out of it. In fairness, I dressed up the proposal rather well. The Queen had ascended to the throne in the previous year (this was now 1954) and was making her first round the world trip in the new Royal Yacht, Britannia, visiting her overseas dominions and colonies. Her last stop before returning home would be Gibraltar, where she would review the garrison on the narrow isthmus that separate the Rock from Spain. However, the "we want Gibraltar back" campaign by the Spanish Government was at its height and there were rumours that an attack might be made on her life by Falangist extremists. The crack reporters of Fleet Street would be on their way to report all of this. And I would be among them.

So off I went, Spanish dictionary in my pocket and my clunking, 40-year-old portable typewriter at my side. I called in at Madrid on the way to do my Franco interview but, strangely, the Dictator – who, of course, had not replied to my letters – refused to see me. I contented myself with doing a graphic Sefton Delmer type colour piece about the mood in the Spanish capital and moved on down to join the Fleet Street circus in Gibraltar.

Two of the top foreign correspondents – Stephen Harper of the Express and Steve Richman of the Herald – had, like me, arrived a little early and they took me under their wing. The three of us trawled the brothels of La Linea, just across the Spanish border, drinking with the girls but not, I hasten to add, sampling the goods, and having a splendid time. They let me see their copy – as a provincial journo I was not, of course, any competition to them – and I cobbled together my own version of the rumours and counter rumours that were circulating at the Rock at that time. I managed to get a bit of a scoop: an interview with the Chief Minister of the Rock, who had been rather overlooked by the great by-liners. He gave me the Gibraltarians' view of the Spaniards, then little reported, and I was pleased, on return home, to find that most of my stuff had been used.

The Queen's visit came and went without incident but I shall never forget watching, from the top of the Rock, the tiny Britannia enter harbour, with a goodly proportion of the British Mediterranean fleet, dressed overall, of course, surrounding her, and sending up to me the sound of sirens and horns pooping to welcome her in. Later, I stood in the Press compound on the landing strip of the isthmus as the Queen reviewed the assembled troops. She looked so fragile, so young and so damned pretty! There was no attack on her, of course. In ways both literal and metaphorical, it would have been an act of *lèse majesté* if an attempt had been made. I remember thinking, who on earth would have wanted to crush such a beautiful butterfly, anyway?

Speaking of beautiful butterflies, I had by then been married for a year. Betty Longfield, the red haired, rather older girl that I had met on the committee of the old scholars association of the ACS, had been "my girl" since the middle of my army service. She has stayed that way ever since. But it was a great treat when I was allowed to tack on my two weeks annual holiday allowance at the end of my Spanish trip and Betty flew out. We spent a second honeymoon at a then unknown little fishing village on the Costa Brava, called Tamariu, experiencing a somnolent Spain that the airlines and the great travel companies were soon to change for ever.

I returned to the daily round of what had become rather a grind for me. A few months before the Spanish trip, I had been made Municipal Correspondent for the Gazette. It was the nearest a provincial daily reporter got to becoming a parliamentary reporter and a position on the paper of great responsibility, for Birmingham, then as now, was a teeming city, with a very active political life both within and outside the council chamber. In addition – as I have alluded to earlier – the great Manzoni re-construction of the city was under way. There was plenty to write about and, at 23, I was ridiculously young to hold the post. Its previous incumbent had been a man of forty plus.

But the minutia of municipal politics bored me and I itched to return to the happy variety of being just a news reporter, albeit one who was often given the juiciest features to write. In terms of age, I was still a junior, but had long since proved myself. Even so, I was amazed when the News Editor took me on one side to inform me that the Chief Reporter was leaving to better himself in Fleet Street and that my great friend, Liam Hunter, would be getting the job. It had been a tough decision, he explained, to choose between Hunter and myself but the fact that he had two years more experience than me had narrowly shaved it. I was genuinely surprised because

I had no idea that I would be in contention and, frankly, I was not sure that I would have been ready, even if offered the post.

Writing of Liam Hunter reminds me that part of the pleasure of being a Gazette reporter was that I worked with some of the finest journalists of the day. Brian Thompson was my first Chief Reporter and he went on to become the Chief Reporter of the News Chronicle in Fleet Street and, later, Marketing Director of European Ferries and my life-long friend. Anne Lloyd-Williams, a hard drinking, hard smoking and dedicated reporter frightened the pants off me. She went on to work on the Daily Mirror, but died tragically early with a brain tumour. Monty Court was a bouncing, brash and supremely confident journalist, with plenty to be confident about. His move to the Evening News in London created the Chief Reporter's vacancy that Liam filled. Monty rose to be News Editor of the Daily Mail and, later, Editor of Sporting Life, a position which fitted him like a glove, given his love of all sport and of racing in particular. I attended his 80th birthday party luncheon in London the other day when the Great and the Good of the Turf came to pay tribute to him.

Also at that lunch was Michael Green, a Gazette sub in my time, not a reporter. Mike loved sport too and rose to fame as the author of the hilariously funny books: The Art of Coarse Rugby, The Art of Coarse Sailing, the Art of Coarse Acting et al. His two books of autobiography were best sellers – and, bless him, he is still writing.

Nor were the district men bereft of character either. Harry Tromans was about 6ft 5ins tall, some fifteen stone in weight and he bestrode his patch – Dudley, to the west of Birmingham – like a colossus in more ways than one. Harry had his district completely sewn up so that nothing newsworthy happened in it, it seemed, before the protagonist rang the Gazette man to tell him first. Certainly, the old Council House in the town was like his back parlour in that he was supremely at home with a succession of aldermen, councillors and Town Clerks – until one evening. After a particularly convivial evening with the Mayor, Harry retired to the mayoral loo. It was a particularly long session for there had been much to eat and drink and, when Harry rose, he found that the door was jammed. Worse than that, everyone had gone home. Harry applied his considerable weight to the door but, being made of stout oak, to high Victorian municipal standards, it resisted all his efforts. No one heard his cries. He was found by the cleaner next morning, on his knees, using the last of his matches in an attempt to burn down the door.

Presiding like a ringmaster over the cast of creative characters in the reporters' room throughout my time was Don Horobin. An incredibly handsome man, slim, with chiselled features, he had the keenest nose for news of any man I have ever met. He could sniff a story buried deeply in even the most innocuous down page paragraph in a local weekly. Not only that, however, he knew exactly how to write it. The most important part of any story, of course, is the beginning. The reader must be engaged immediately. Leaning over your shoulder as you typed, Don would sigh and say, "No cocker. The intro point is down here. Bring that up. Lead with it."

Years later, when running my own business, I was to think back many times to Horobin and his talent for knowing *what mattered*. When considering an abstruse problem surrounded by a mass of seemingly important points, all crying out to be given priority, I found myself often thinking, "what would Don say? Which would he point to and say, 'this is the intro, cocker, bring it up.'" Don left the Midlands for London eventually to become Deputy News Editor at Independent Television News, in its great days. When he died a memorial service was held for him in St Bride's, Fleet Street. There, a message was read out from Rupert Murdoch, the great media mogul in New York. It said, simply: "Horobin was the best journalist I ever knew."

Throughout 1955, increasingly bored by the municipal round, I tried hard to find a job in Fleet Street. I was choosy. I could perhaps have made it to The Mirror or the Sketch, but I eschewed the tabloids. With a conceit which perhaps sat ill with my young years, I wanted to join "a serious newspaper." But it was a bad time, with a series of strikes having hit the news publishers and costs were being cut. "Try again later," I was told. I had a happy relationship with most of the reporters on the Birmingham Post and one or two of them urged me to apply for a reporter's post there which had become available. More in frustration than conviction, I applied and was offered the job.

It was more money and back to what I loved – the daily round of being a general news reporter. The Post's style, of course, was markedly different. It was serious and more heavy in content. But, once there, I was surprised to find that the writing style was more liberal. The Gazette, under the stern news eye of Horobin, drove the story on. The Post allowed you to develop your story with more flexibility. One elderly reporter (most of the Post's men were considerably older than the Gazette's) even began one piece with the words: "Queen Ann is indubitably dead…" And this on the news pages! Blimey!!

I enjoyed the short time I was on the Post. People were friendly, courteous, and the pace less frenetic. But I itched still for London. When the call came, though, it was from a most unexpected quarter.

Jack Hill was the Daily Express's Midlands reporter, a man of immense charm and charisma – and an ex Gazette man. He told me that the Public Relations Officer of the Rootes Group, then the third largest of the country's motor manufacturers and makers of Humber, Hillman, Sunbeam and Singer cars, plus Commer trucks, was looking for a bright journalist to join his team in London. I was a bit young but he thought I stood a good chance, because the PRO was John Bullock, a former Chief Reporter of the Gazette. Ah, the Mafia was in action...!

I took a train to the big city and met Bullock in Devonshire House, the Group's immensely impressive headquarters in Piccadilly. He was charm personified, handsome with an unfashionable centre parting and prematurely grey hair. He had a warm sense of humour and a happy turn of phrase – the PR man personified. (He still is.) He offered me the job at £950 a year and I accepted. I was back in London.

Chapter 12

BRIGHT LIGHTS
AND DARK MILLS

I must begin this chapter with a word or two about "public relations." It is a phrase which has now entered the language as meaning, I guess, the smoothing of relationships, the building of a situation which helps selling, whether that be of a political manifesto or a product to the consumer. In fact, the phrase itself has mutated into something small, sharper and even less favourable: spin. In my understanding now, that word means lying. The practitioners are less smooth, although no less plausible. They can be hard men who bully politicians from *inside* their party and, from a position of power, put pressure on the media in a similar intransigent and often unscrupulous way.

Well! It was not like that in my day…

Concerns and institutions, whether commercial or not, established the need for PR practitioners because they felt they could not handle the needs of the media – initially the Press, of course – who demanded answers to questions quickly to match their deadlines and who could themselves be unscrupulous in phrasing questions and reporting the answers. Someone was needed, it was clear, who could *understand* the needs of the Press and be a vital link between the media and management, handling the needs of both sides in a competent and ethical way.

Back in the mid fifties, then, PR was respectable. Certainly it was a career that was attractive to journalists, for, in addition to demanding their particular skills and knowledge "of the trade," it paid much more and it promised a life style of some affluence beyond the pay packet, involving as it did liberal expense accounts and the need to cultivate senior people in the media. In addition to journalistic ability, then, one was expected to have social skills and, if one could manage it, a touch of charm.

That was the world I entered and where, with the Rootes Group, I stayed for the next eight years. In that time, I learned a lot about the manufacturing industry upon which Britain then depended, but also how to handle head waiters, match a decent wine to even more decent food, and which night clubs had the best floor shows (in those days, the Embassy Club in Bond Street, without a doubt). Betty and I went to live in the country, just outside Tunbridge Wells, in Kent, where two lovely children, Alison and Paul were born, in 1956 and 1959 respectively. The commuting was hell but London was, then as now, fascinating and the bright lights burned all around me.

They glowed even more brightly when, after serving under John Bullock for five years, I took his job as Group Public Relations Officer, when he left to join the board of a PR agency and then to start his own business. I inherited a staff which included my old chum Liam Hunter, who had followed me down from the Birmingham Gazette, and John Rowe, who came from a technical journal background and who, apart from being the most genial and trustworthy of men, knew about "the bloody cars." Much of my time through all the years, was spent in writing speeches and ghosting articles for the members of the Rootes family who owned and ran the business. Lord Rootes – Billy Rootes, a man of boundless energy and gift for making money as well as motor cars – was the dominant figure, of course. The trouble was that, although a supremely confident and hugely respected elder statesman, with a rather raffish reputation, he did not speak well in public on formal occasions and had a poor sense of humour.

In drafting yet another speech for him when he was Chairman of the Dollar Exports Council, I endeavoured to liven up the blasted thing by inserting a joke – not a good joke, but a joke nevertheless. It went like this: "The man who says that we can't sell British goods to the USA doesn't know what he's talking about. He probably thinks that a metronome is some dwarf in the Paris underground…"

The draft went upstairs, where Billy sat in some state in what we called "The Green Belt," in an office next door to his younger brother and partner, Sir Reginald. Within minutes I was summoned. Glowering over his spectacles he waved the speech and said, "what's this about a dwarf?"

"Oh, it's just an attempt to liven the speech up, a bit," I muttered. "Leave it out if you don't think it's funny."

"It's bloody silly," he said. "A metronome is one of those things," he moved his finger, "that goes tick tock, tick tock."

"I know, sir. But it's a play on words, you see…"

"Don't know what you're talking about. Come with me."

He stalked to Sir Reginald's door and flung it open. "Here, Reggie," he called. "What's a metronome?"

Sir Reginald, the quiet one of the two and an distinguished ex-Civil Servant, lifted his eyebrows, put down his spectacles and he, too, waved his finger. "It's one of those things that goes, tick tock, tick tock, isn't it?"

"There you are, I told him so." Lord Rootes whirled on me. "This bloody fool says it's a dwarf."

I knew then that I really had to move on. It wasn't only the banality of working for people whom I really didn't respect (there was a demeaning air of feudality about it, too, for we were expected to refer to the brothers' sons as "Mr Geoffrey", "Mr Brian" and "Mr Timothy"), but my job was becoming more and more involved in handling the publicity that surrounded the growing number of strikes that were beginning to cripple the business. So many of them seemed to break out on the weekend shift and I was rarely left in peace on Saturdays and Sundays down in Tunbridge Wells.

The National Union of Vehicle Builders were mainly involved, although there were others, and it gradually occurred to me that most of the stoppages were frivolous and that some deeper, strategic motivation lay beyond them. As the son of a Communist and one who still clung to his leftist credentials, I was reluctant to think that these events were part of a long term plan to bring down the British motor industry. But as I grew more deeply involved, I realised that the British Communist Party was indeed behind most, if not all, of the strikes.

The longest and the one that, in the end, brought the Rootes Group to its knees, occurred in 1963 at British Light Steel Pressings, one of the Group's most important manufacturing units based in west London. That strike – its Genesis is lost to me now – was run impeccably from a small Communist Party office in Acton. Its organising committee included its own Press Officer – and boy, wasn't he efficient! I would have been proud to have him on my staff. Part of the difficulty I faced was that most of the industrial correspondents reporting on the strike were left leaning, in political terms. This meant that, although they certainly did not distort the facts, their basic sympathies were towards the workers and not the employers, particularly the Rootes family who were regarded, I suspect, as dinosaurs, running a family business in an age of big industrial units. We won, however, in the end and the strike collapsed. Yet the cost was astronomical, for all of the Group's factories had to close while the dispute continued. A couple of years later, the Group was sold to Chrysler.

Through the eight months or so that the strike was continuing I never once told a lie or a half truth in handling the dozens of calls from the media that came in every day. I *did not spin*. At its end, I received a formal letter from the Guild of Industrial Editors, expressing their thanks for my honesty and help to them during the long dispute. I treasured that. I heard nothing from the Rootes family.

So it was that I jumped at the chance when Betty handed me a Sunday Times cutting in 1963. A Public Relations Manager was wanted for an international organisation based in London. There would be much foreign travel involved. I went through a series of interviews with the headhunters and with my prospective employer.

The organisation was the International Wool Secretariat. At first I baulked. I had only dimly heard of it (those "there is no substitute for wool" rhymes on tube cards) and the word Secretariat was off-putting, to say the least. But I was persuaded to go through the interviewing process by the head hunter – well, I thought, it would be good experience, at least, for I had been out of the job market for some years and I had certainly had enough of the Rootes Group. As I progressed through the interviews, however, I became more intrigued. This IWS represented the wool growers of Australia, New Zealand and South Africa and its leaders were embarked on an ambitious programme to find a £13million annual budget to mount a direct attack on the synthetic fibres that were stealing their traditional markets. This would involve establishing some thirty branches in countries throughout the world and launching a definitive trade mark for wool, the Woolmark. A strong public relations programme was part of the strategy and I would be expected to set up and oversee a network of PR operations in these markets.

The clincher came for me when I had my final interview with the IWS's Managing Director. William Vines was an Australian (with, I learned later, a Mention in Despatches from fighting the Japanese). Then in his late thirties, tall, slim, and with his clipped moustache, he looked a cross between David Niven and Clark Gable. He was affable but to the point and asked me the right sort of questions. As ex-managing director of an international paint company, he even knew Billy Rootes. I got the job and I knew that I was going to work for someone I respected. That never changed.

The years that followed were the happiest since my early days at the Birmingham Gazette. I travelled hard and worked hard, appointing good PR practicioners in the new branches and establishing a strategy for our work. We launched the Woolmark – a ground-breaking trade-mark which certified the fibre content of the cloth or garment bearing it and certain performance standards for the product – and even got the Pope to bless it in the Vatican!

To back up the extensive consumer advertising that surrounded the mark, we hatched a series of publicity innovations. By far the most successful of these was our sponsorship of Sir Francis Chichester in his circumnavigation of the globe. We were looking for some way of thrusting the mark forward in unusual but not illogical situations. For instance, painting the Woolmark on a hot air balloon attempting to cross the Atlantic might attract attention but it would be just another billboard. Backing a great sailor in his attempt to be the first man to sail in the wake of the great wool sailing clippers, the "wrong way round the world," however, would be logical, particularly if we gave him shrink resistant sweaters to wear and permanently creased (on one leg only) trousers, in a test of the new technologies involved. We made Chichester's boat, Gypsy Moth IV, in fact, a kind of floating wool test bed. (The sweaters were fine but all creases in the trousers had gone on Francis's return, which is just as well, because –

ahem – we forgot to record which leg was creased conventionally and the other by the new technology).

It had been my deputy, Nigel Cole – another from the great Birmingham Gazette hothouse and now a lifetime friend – who had sussed out that Chichester's great venture, would be stillborn unless he received financial backing. In negotiating with Francis we had a series of delightful lunches with him during one of which he suggested that, instead, of merely handing over the money, we should share the ownership of the boat, actually buying part of it, thus enabling us to insure our share.

"You'd be wise to do this," he observed wryly over his glass of Puligny-Montrachet, "because, while I'm a bloody good navigator, I'm not the best sailor in the world and I might hit the Isle of Wight. Then you would get your money back."

In his working up trials, he hit the Isle of Wight.

The damage was slight and no-one could really doubt his sailing ability, of course. His voyage, with the new Woolmark on his prow and on his sailing cap, made him internationally famous and earned him a knighthood. It also boosted the recognition of our mark hugely throughout the world, at a time when we were pushing hard to get it established. I not-at-all humbly submit that this was one of the first and certainly most successful examples of sponsorship to be carried out in the UK.

It helped to earn me promotion, for before Bill Vines left to resume a hugely successful business career in Australia (as I write, he is still alive, in his nineties, now Sir William and the holder of a coveted Order of Australia) he plucked me out of public relations work and put me into line management, as the IWS's UK Branch Director. It was a huge step for me because I immediately had to become a businessman, rather than a publicist, responsible for wool consumption in the UK and handling a staff of 120, including technicians; marketers in end products ranging from couture gowns to carpets and furnishing fabrics; trade mark experts; advertising men and women; a fashion adviser; and the usual back up of office administrators and accountants. For someone who hardly knew the difference between the weft and warp it was a formidable challenge and I had to step warily. Everyone on my staff, it seemed, was an expert but me.

The job involved facing up to the great wool barons of Yorkshire, who were being daily wooed by the synthetic fibre manufacturers, with all the backing of the great chemical companies. We were outspent but we were determined not to be out-marketed and I plunged into a round of visits throughout Yorkshire and Scotland. The bright lights and night clubs of the motor industry days were now a distant memory and many of those mills were certainly dark, although certainly not satanic. Wool processing, of course, was one of Britain's oldest industries. From its initial sorting and carding as a raw material, through the various operations of spinning, weaving or knitting, into garment or carpet making, it was a highly complex business and I had to deal with what seemed like a myriad different mini-industries, each with its own technologies and vocabularies. It was our job to try and put pressure on them all – including the big retailers like the mighty Marks and Spencers, who called the final tune.

It was a big stretch for an ex-news reporter and I struggled at first. Thank God I had the help of a good staff, of whom Colin Rennie, an ex-synthetic fibre man and my Marketing Manager, and, later Tony Gould, were outstanding.

The tools we used were varied and were applied at various stages of the processing line. These included technical support for the mills; the introduction of new technology to add modern performance attributes, such as machine washability in knitwear, to support the fibre's magnificent age old qualities; a strong fashion service to ensure that wool processors kept up to date with colour and garment trends; marketing pressures, such as the offer of advertising funds to support the end-users; our own strong consumer advertising, which included highly creative television work; and, above all, the power of the Woolmark, offering a guarantee of policed quality to its licensees.

It was fascinating work, controlling all of these activities and juggling budgets to compete with such huge competitors as Courtaulds and ICI Fibres. I learned so much that was miles away, of course, from news rooms and PR lunches. And the man from whom I learned the most was my first Managing Director, Bill Vines. I stayed with the IWS for seventeen hugely fulfilling years, but Vines was there for only my first five. Yet – as with Horobin years before – he impressed me so much, in his case with his business acumen, man-management skills, fairness and honesty and, of course, I pinched many of his little touches: such as, at the beginning of the many, many meetings that I chaired each month, stating at the beginning "the business of this meeting is to further and improve our technical service skills," or whatever. It set the tone.

He had a reputation for his high ethical standards. It was rumoured that when once his wife forget to declare at customs the packets of cigarettes she had put away in her case, he gently made her retrace her steps and declare them. I had a painful experience of my own in this regard. I had made a (for once) reasonably good speech at an international wool conference in Portugal. It impressed one of the quality cloth manufacturers of Italy who, as a result, sent me a suit length of his very expensive cloth on my return to London. I was admiring it in my office when the boss's PA came through the door to say that, as Mr Vines had also received the gift of a suit length from the same source, perhaps our two letters of thanks – *with our cheques for the cloth* – could go together? It was Vines's typically gentle way of reminding me that, in our position, we always had to be above reproach. Mind you, I could have so done with that suit..!

In due course, I was promoted again at the IWS and became an Area Director, one down from the top job. I controlled branches in Northern Europe, including the

UK, of course, and our embryonic operations in South America. It gave a new dimension to the work in that, as part of top management, I had to help to frame policy and was at more of a distance from the market place. It was a role I was less happy with, because, of course, it was far less "hands on." The work of establishing an IWS operation and acquiring Woolmark licencees in South America was challenging, though. It had its bizarre moments, as when I was visiting a mill in Columbia, near Bogata, run by a smooth, Harvard-educated Columbian.

The Managing Director was proudly showing me his latest acquisitions, a brace of high speed, Swiss made looms. As I stood with him admiring the speed at which the fine wool cloth was being woven I noticed that the selvedge – that's the line at the bottom of each piece of cloth that denotes its origin – was weaving the words, "woven in Huddersfield, UK." He looked sheepish. "We have to do it," he said, "because fine wool cloth is just not associated with Columbia."

I swallowed hard. The man was a big user of Australian wool and I was there as a wool salesman, not a policeman. "Okay," I said, "but don't you dare put our Woolmark on a woolblend cloth."

I was now in my late forties and positioned in that tight little triangle of top management that every company creates at the tip of its pyramid of manpower. A new Managing Director was created – a Ph.D from the Bronx, New York – and my face didn't fit. I therefore left the IWS at a time of great personal unhappiness for me, of which more later.

The wool trade was declining and I had skills and salary expectations that were difficult to place in formal employment. So I set up my brass plate as a marketing consultant in textiles. To my amazement, companies came knocking on my door and I spent the next three years on my own (or at least with the indefatigable Betty back home as Deputy Chairman, PA, typist and Keeper Up of Morale), travelling throughout the UK and twice around the world for companies that included Datsun, the International Trade Centre in Geneva, News International, Shetland Islands Council, the British Wool Marketing Board and the British Clothing Industry Economic Development Council. During this time I also served as chairman of the Retail Trading Association.

But as a one man band, I had nothing to sell on if and when the time came to retire, so that when the last opportunity came knocking on the door I was more than ready to open it wide. The company was the Lonsdale Advertising Group, one of the oldest and best established in London, who were looking for a new Managing Director for one its subsidiary companies, Osborne Marketing Communications. We were happy to get together and, before long, I had bought equity in it and we became Lonsdale Wilcox Ltd.

Much of the work was PR oriented and so I was back, to some extent, to where I started. I enjoyed re-building the company and we acquired clients that included the Burton Group, many of Courtaulds' clothing brand names, the Shetland Islands, Case Tractors, the tourists boards of Malta and Gibraltar (back to the Rock after forty years!) and the Falkland Islands Development Corporation. During most of this time I was non-executive chairman of Wilcox, Brown and Madden, a textile-based technical and marketing consultancy formed by old IWS colleagues.

As I worked hard, servicing the clients and keeping our companies in the black (successfully, I am glad to say), I began more and more to wish to turn the clock back and write – not journalism but books and, if I could manage it, novels. All through my business life I had tried to write short stories and had had plenty of professional articles published in a wide variety of media. But success in fiction escaped me. It was bad enough trying to be creative when, as on holiday, one seemed to have all the time in the world, but trying to write while employed full time and, in particular, running a business, I found extremely difficult. I had (and still do) so much admiration for those writers like Fay Weldon who knocked out best sellers at the kitchen table after cooking the family dinner and putting the children to bed.

So it was that, when the opportunity occurred to sell the business and take my share out of it, I jumped at the chance. Going the whole hog, we also sold our flat in Belgravia (not as swish as it sounds, as it was rather on the lower slopes, but, dammit, it was still Belgravia!) and moved to the country. We found a cottage in South West Wiltshire and, in a studio at the bottom of the garden, among the fairies, I began to write.

I am still there, seventeen years later, having now published two books of non fiction, seven works of fiction in the Simon Fonthill series and an autobiography.

So I look back now with affection at a happy childhood and, with a touch of pride at an extremely varied and moderately successful career, ending now, as I always wished it would, as an author and novelist. Nevertheless, there was an event in my life which has always hung over this narrative and to which I have referred obliquely. I must turn to it now so that the story is complete. I have kept it discrete because it somehow seems to stand alone and I need a bit of space to relate it fully. In telling this part of my story I have, for many different reasons, deleted the names of many of the people in it and also that of the university involved.

It occurred on 1st May 1979 when our dear son Paul hanged himself.

Part III
THE STORY OF PAUL

Chapter 13

THE HOW OF IT

About eighteen months after Paul's death, I was approached by Peter Jackson, then as now a very good friend from my days as a journalist, who was then editing a mass circulation weekly magazine. He asked me to write the story of Paul's suicide as part of a series called "Second Opinion" the magazine was running. Wondering whether I was up to it, I demurred at first, then agreed. The finished piece appeared on 18th October 1980. Looking at it again, thirty years later, it seems as good a way as any to relay what happened in a reasonably concise form, so I reproduce it below.

Paul died, as far as we know, some time during the early afternoon of May 1, 1979. He was found hanging from a high branch of a tree, deep in the less frequented part of a wood near the university where he was a first year student. He was just 20 and he had taken his own life.

These are almost the only facts we have. The rest of the story, including the motivation, is an unsatisfactory mixture of speculation and post-rationalisation. The temptation for us now, some 18 months on, is to say wearily that it doesn't matter anyway. He's gone and the rest is arid.

Will it help others to know? Is suicide – real suicide, that is, not the cry-for-help attempt which ends with a stomach pump – telegraphed in advance to the point where friends and family can act on the warning signs? Sometimes, perhaps, but not in our case. That is why this story, as a cautionary tale, will probably fail. But let's tell it and see.

Paul was born in March 1959 into an unremarkable family. He followed his sister Alison by two and half years and they grew up fighting each other and then, as brothers and sisters often do, loving each other warmly, if unspokenly, as their teens brought companionship and respect.

A little surprisingly, he became a leader at prep school (his headmaster wrote remembering him as a "highly successful" head boy, with a great sense of humour) and he progressed smoothly to the local public school as a day pupil. Here, the pattern was unremarkable, except that even a parent striving for objectivity has to admit that he was popular. The telephone at home never stopped ringing. After his death the school held a special memorial service and the headmaster said: "Paul was a cheerful boy with a sunny disposition who made friends easily and very much enjoyed life… Perhaps he shone most as a games player – the first rugby XV; in cricket, a first XI bowler with a deceptive in-swing which gained him many wickets; a good hockey player. He enjoyed acting, too, and altogether he made good use of his many talents. What I remember most about him is his cheerful good humour and a very infectious enthusiasm. He put a lot into his short life and got a lot out of it…"

Paul gained 11 "O" levels without much effort and three "A's" with considerable effort, for girls had become important by then. Reluctantly, at my request, he stayed for an extra term to study for Oxbridge, but he decided not to finish the course. He was accepted at a provincial university and occupied the waiting time before going up by portering in a local hospital and then, for seven months, working in Paris.

He seemed to enjoy France and distinguished himself in Paris on a night out with old school friends by raising a glass or two and then falling into the brown, swollen Seine and being swept along for 200 metres before scrambling ashore, breathless with terror and laughter. They then all returned to a café, Paul dripping over the crepes, to try another bottle.

All very normal and high spirited. At about this time, however, we had deducted deeper qualities in him – qualities perhaps even a little fey. We found, for instance, that he had once played truant in the sixth form at school. This was at a time when his closest friend had hit hard drugs and been in a hallucinatory state for several days. Paul sat alone in a local park for two days and thought it all through.

Drugs were not really for him. He had smoked marijuana at parties but, according to his sister (much more of a confidante than his parents, of course) they did little for him. The drinking, too, seemed fairly conventional and confined mainly to a few pints in the Pigeon Pair.

In his first term at university he did well and enjoyed the work. After Christmas, he seemed less happy, although not worryingly so. He confessed that he felt under-used and doubted the value of the analysis of philosophy and literature which was now his daily round. But it was all very rationally expressed. A young mind stretching itself.

Then, with Spring on its way, he put down his pen in mid-essay, walked two miles – picking up a length of clothes line on the way – pushed his way through deep undergrowth and hanged himself. It seemed he smoked a last cigarette, but there was no note, only a faintly-decipherable phrase in ball-point on one finger: "Easier this way."

My wife and I were away at the time, visiting our daughter Alison at university in Germany. The day Paul died was an extremely happy one for us, in fact. The three of us tramped high above the snow line in the mountains of the Black Forest with cheeks tingling and conversation flowing. "Wouldn't Paul have loved this," we said more than once. So much for extra-sensory perception!

At the inquest, a college friend revealed that, two days before his death, Paul had sat alone in a field and contemplated suicide. But the sun shone and the grass was green and he resolved to live and plunge back into his work. That resolve didn't last long.

Why did he do it? We don't know and we never will now. His death was a complete and brutal shock to us. Did we really know him? Well, of course, we knew a strong, vital part of him, the part which we believed to be all — or most — of him. But there was another Paul we discovered after his death.

In an old scrap-book there is a diary entry for 1.30 a.m., Thursday October 16, 1976: "I have just achieved strength — passed a test of will. Proved myself to myself. I now know I can. I did it! I threw myself down the stairs! It took at least half an hour of confused thought and self-persuasion. I feel like I've just reached the summit of Everest…"

There is poetry, too. Very contemporary, sometimes original verses, sitting in an old exercise book in sad juxtaposition with French transitive verbs. Self-critically, he dismisses one of his efforts as, "a relic of useless thought-shrines."

His mind, then, was becoming very sensitised by the time he went to university. In his second term there, Paul opted to take a course entitled "The Absurd." This was an analysis of some of the recent great writings on the meaning of existence and the validity, among other things, of suicide. He was writing an essay on Albert Camus's novel, The Outsider, *when he interrupted it to take his last walk.*

It is hard to believe that this concentrated dose of Camus and Kafka did not have some effect on Paul's already highly-tuned view of mortality. After the inquest, where the university authorities had declined to say that they would reconsider the contents of the course for first-year students, I argued with them. I also queried their standards of pastoral care for young students.

In a correspondence which was non-acrimonious and thoughtful (their efforts and care when Paul was first missed were exemplary), they contended that the content of the course was not depressive but was necessary stuff for students tackling the great truths. They also predictably reminded me of the difficulties of monitoring the movements of hundreds of young people living independent lives on campus.

So there we are. Our son had become a suicide statistic. Amazingly, astoundingly, it had happened to us.

Paul did not seem to go wrong. There was no failure, or obvious burden, no disastrously broken love affair. His depression, if depression there was, was not carried manically for all to see. In fact, the Coroner refused to record any disturbance of the balance of mind. Paul's death, he said simply in his verdict, was self-inflicted, by hanging.

I still worry about the weight and rather macabre content of that course he was studying, but I find it difficult to draw real lessons from the tragedy. Two points only emerge with relative clarity.

The first is that we all live our lives at different levels and it is the hidden strata of existence that can sometimes be the most important. We knew that Paul was intelligent, but we only learned from his personal writings later just how vividly and critically he viewed the daily absurdities of life. His very private, interior life was lived on a far more sensitive and judgmental plane than that which he presented to the world. Even we, who loved him and whom he loved reciprocally, were not aware of this.

The second point leads from the first. I believe that Paul made a choice and that he had a right to make it, hurtful and rejecting as it was to the rest of us. So we have no resentment about him. He lives on in our hearts, poised on top of the stairs, trying to pluck up courage to jump to prove to himself something or other.

The story of Paul could end there, of course, but there is more to say – a touch more on The How of It, much more on the Why of It and a final twist in The End of It.

My article produced a handful of letters from parents who had recently suffered in the same way. Most of them merely wanted to empathise with us and share their pain but one or two were more bleak, showing that time did not seem in their case to have produced its healing balm – and, indeed, not auguring well for us in this regard. I tried to help as best I could (the blind leading the blind!), replying to them all and had one further letter back from the husband of the original writer. He wrote frankly of his wife's continuing distress, despite the fact that they had three other, happy children, but he also said that the article had given them both great comfort and, referring to my letter to his wife, closed by writing, "But you might be pleased to hear that your phrase, 'perhaps she had something of greater moment to do elsewhere' has helped more than anything I have been able to say to her in the last two and half years…" In a strange, "may-I-borrow-your-crutch-please" kind of way, his tribute did more than most things that had happened since Paul's death to cheer me up. It seemed that, after all, I was still able to be useful to *someone*, if not to my son when he had needed me.

The pain of his death to us, of course, was immediate: shocking and deeply wounding. It seems that he had gone missing from college on the morning of Tuesday 1st May but that the alarm was not given until the following Saturday, when a party of students was immediately mustered to begin the search for him. On that day, I was playing cricket in Banstead, Surrey, and was taking the first refreshing beer in the pavilion at the end of the match when I was called to the telephone, to be told by Betty that she had just heard that Paul was missing. I immediately drove back to our home, now in Islington, London, and we spent a silent evening and the following morning, hardly engaging in eye contact with each other, while our minds raced over the possibilities of his disappearance. Neither of us, for one moment, thought that he would have taken his own life. He was just not that sort of boy. Perhaps work had got him down, or, more likely, he'd fallen out with the girl with whom he was sharing a flat and gone on walkabout to clear his head. But a rope and a tree…? Never!

Our anxiety mounted, however, as the hours went by and all speculation ended when the white faced policewoman knocked on the door. Neither Betty nor I can recall in detail what followed after that; it is most likely that we have both erased it from our mind and we both have no wish now to pick at that memory scab. Somehow we drove down to the university town and were given a bed for the night by good friends nearby. Luckily, we did not have to identify the body, for that had been done by the university authorities, but we did have to collect his belongings (apart from those kept for the Coroner) and, of course, meet an undertaker.

However, there is one person who stands out from those foggy, somnambulistic hours at the university. To our shame, neither Betty nor I can now remember his name, but he was the college chaplain, who gave us quiet, authoritative but sympathetic and quite unemotional sympathy. We clung to this young man as shipwrecked mariners cling to a storm-swept rock and from the time and care he devoted to us no-one could have known that his own father had died only a couple of days before. Betty's faith, although a little faint at this time, had never quite departed her, but I had embraced agnosticism soon after putting down my choirboy's cassock. As a result, my spinning brain could find no intellectual succour. Worse. Wasn't there something in the teachings of the Christian church that said that suicides could never enter the Kingdom of Heaven – if there was one, that is? Would our dear son be forced to bugger about as a boatman on the dreaded River Styx, or in some other unsanctified territory, for all eternity? I deride the thought now, but it seemed real to me in those nightmare hours. Our Rock, however, disabused me of such nonsense. Paul, he said, was at that moment, sitting next to the Chaplain's own father in heaven. Even now, in much calmer waters and thirty years after the event, I can recall the relief that flooded through me. If it is a just world, that young man should shortly appear on our screens as he is enthroned as the next white-haired Archbishop of Canterbury. I only hope that Betty and I recognise him.

The chapel at the crematorium was packed for the short service. Everyone from Paul's short life, it seemed, had come to pay tribute. There was nothing hole and corner, "suicide is a sin," about the event and the Chaplain in his address, at my request, repeated his assurance that Paul was joined with his own father on the right hand of someone or other in the Ethereal Upstairs. Although painful and, alas in my case, ridiculously tearful, it was a strangely heart-warming occasion, reminding us just how much Paul was loved and liked by everyone. It was by no means a farewell to a poor, twisted soul. This was a boy who led the pack, who featured twice in successive years in the cricketer's Wisden for topping his school's bowling averages, and who had girl friends galore.

The last of them we hardly knew. We were not quite sure whether this sharing of a flat off-campus idea with her sprang from a love affair or from economic necessity. Having met her, we rather veered to the latter. She gave evidence at the inquest (of which more later) and, days later, when the fuss had subsided somewhat, we journeyed down again to buy her lunch and see if she could shed a little more light on the tragedy. She did her best but could not be more forthcoming. Yes, Paul had seemed depressed and had talked about suicide a few days before the event, saying that he lacked self confidence and "hadn't any feelings to enjoy life." But then, on the day before his death, he had told her that he was going to bury himself in his work.

"Lacked confidence?" This didn't sound like our son, but then, as I wrote in the article, it is the hidden strata of a person's existence that is often the most important.

It was at roughly this time, when we drove down for the last time to pick up Paul's clothing, that – in the moment of putting his so well-remembered jeans, with the leather belt I bought him in Uruguay, his shirt, socks and boots – into the boot of the car that I lost it. A fierce rage consumed me, making me react this time not with tears but with anger at the agony and sheer waste of it all – at the squandering of his years and of our love for him – and I hurled the garments into the car, shouting and swearing at the top of my voice. Students passing gave me a wide berth but I didn't care. I got into the car, slammed the door and drove away from the university very, very fast.

The inquest itself was a miserable affair, of course. Betty wisely chose not to come but I was accompanied by two of my oldest chums, Nigel Cole and Bryan Thompson. I had tried to dissuade them from giving up a day's work, telling them that I would be quite composed on my own. In fact, I became hugely grateful for their presence by the time the proceedings had finished.

The grisly, forensic part was difficult for me. Evidence was given that there were no signs of drugs in Paul's digestive system, that he was a perfectly healthy young man and that his act had seemed to be coolly premeditated, in that he had stolen a clothes line from a back garden, walked for some time into the deepest part of the wood, climbed a tree, fixed the line to a branch and jumped. His neck, however, had not been broken and he had died of asphyxiation. (This latter detail stunned me then and has haunted me ever since. The agony he must have suffered…)

On arrival at the inquest, I had been surprised to find that the university had fielded a large team of academics, who gave evidence concerning the course on "The Absurd" that Paul was taking, and led by a barrister who told the Coroner that the staff felt that the course had not contributed to his death and that the university would not be cancelling it as a result of his suicide. It was, he explained, a very popular part of the syllabus, with some 60 students signed up for it.

Evidence was given that showed that Paul had taken a leading part in the discussion centred on Albert Camus's books, "The Outsider" and "The Myth of Sisyphus." I quote now from the deposition given to the Coroner by the Seminar Leader of the group:

"Paul was the first student to voice an opinion. His argument was that he found the book contradictory since if (as he thought Camus argued) life was judged to be meaningless, then it made no sense to construct a philosophy since to do so was to give a meaning to life. I cannot remember his exact words, but I know that he spoke with the air of someone who has found a flaw in the reasoning of the book he has read and who objects to that rather than with the air of someone who believes that life is meaningless or has been convinced that it is."

Hmmm. I realised then that the university was defending its values but, more than that, it was erecting a defensive lager (with the barrister as commander in chief) against what it perceived might be an attack by me. In fact, I was far too distressed by it all to mount an attack or even ask questions, let alone employ my own lawyer to appear for me. I just wanted to get at the facts. Outside the court, when I had regained my composure, I did approach the formidable varsity team and ask, "surely you did not mean that you are going to continue the course?" Oh yes, they replied. These were important works that should be studied by undergraduates, even those in their first year.

On the long drive home, with my silent companions, I thought long and hard about this.

Chapter 14

THE WHY OF IT

In the weeks following the cremation and then the inquest I also thought deeply about my own relationship with Paul. It plays a part in this story, of course, and I shall refer to it again later. Then, however, I was forced to examine my behaviour towards my son and to dredge through the previous years in an attempt to pick up clues to see whether I had, however unintentionally, helped him to feel alienated towards his family or perhaps just to me.

In the children's early years, it was Alison who caused us most concern, although that is, perhaps, too strong a word to describe the minor irritations she presented to Betty and me. As she grew, she seemed to become morose, even sullen. The contrast to Paul's gaiety was marked and Betty and I had to force ourselves to treat the two equally. In those days, if Paul was a bright, sunny morning, full of promise, Alison was a cloudy afternoon, presaging a rainy evening. Her moments of shared happiness with us were often punctuated by passages of introspection.

(I should insert here that our daughter shed this strange chrysalis towards the end of her teens and has grown up to be a warm, loving and gregarious person. She is now working hard as an export marketer, is a competent linguist with a wide circle of friends and, in a hackneyed phrase, is the light of our lives in these our late years. But this is Paul's story, not hers, and I only include this reference to her early years to show the contrast with her brother in those days.)

So Paul presented no problems. Full of energy and life, he was a delight to his mother and me. As a lover of sport but a very modest practitioner myself, I wallowed in his prowess as a footballer and cricketer at his prep school and then at rugby, cricket and hockey at his public school. I was puzzled, then, that he always avoided playing cricket with me at my club, Banstead, during the school vacation. A swing bowler of talent who topped the averages in the school's first eleven in his freshman year, he would always find an excuse to avoid playing for me when, as captain, I was short of a bowler. Having turned me down, he would sometimes then appear in a lower eleven on the same day, "just to help out at the last minute," as he said. Strange… Would he think that I would be overbearing with him and tell him what to do? What nonsense. But I took no offence and let the matter lie.

Then, as he went through into his late teens, it occurred to me that perhaps we were not talking together as much as we should. He was good at schoolwork and, it seemed, I was never needed to help with his prep at home. He remained, however, close to his mother and a great chum to his sister. Wrapped up in my job, I did not worry too much about all this. I did, however, discuss it briefly with Betty who assured me that there was no rift and we both agreed that I certainly should not make an issue of it with Paul. It was, after all, not unusual for a father to be closer to the daughter and the mother to the son. Quite natural, in fact, and it would all come out in the growing up wash. Of course I loved him dearly but I decided that I would let the boy find his own level with me and not intrude into his life with any kind of parental heavy handedness.

In fact, I was rather proud of the only occasion when I did intervene. When he was fifteen, Paul had had his first relationship with a splendidly good looking girl (she went on to become a professor of medicine) with whom he fell completely in love. When their brief affair ended, at her instigation, it upset him terribly. I learned all about this, of course, from Betty, for Paul remained distant and tearful. It was strange to see him like this but I resisted the strong temptation to joss him out of it by telling him that there would be other girls for him later and that Mary was not the only pebble on the beach. No, doing my best to resist a smile, I gravely advised that he should leave her alone for a while and stay friendly because, I said, she would eventually come round to recognising his worth and that they would come together a little later. His eyes lit up briefly at this and he nodded. "Okay, Dad."

But this was an exception. As his teen years went by, Paul seemed almost shy of me. When he went to Paris, however, (I found him a job there and also a "respectable" place to stay − which he immediately left and ended up living happily in an under-the-stairs tiny room in the Tunisian quarter) I began to attempt a little cautious bonding. I did not rush the process but it seemed an improvement.

That is how things stayed until his death: a relationship almost at arm's length, but one that I felt was slowly, very slowly, getting better. I rationalised that I might have seemed perhaps to be too strong and over-powering to him (faults that I must confess have been levelled at me before and since). But was I partly guilty of his death? Surely not. Even in the deepest moment of my misery I could not believe this − and neither did Betty or Alison. Perhaps if I had made a more conscious effort in his last months to get a little closer it might have helped, but probably not much.

That is how I felt in those months after his death. I will return to the subject later but then I fiercely resisted any feeling of guilt and busied myself digging into what Paul had been doing as background to his university course to help in what I felt would have to be a tussle with the college authorities.

I found, of course, his notebooks with his early poetry and a few scattered diary entries, including that heart-breaking written celebration of his feat in hurling himself down the stairs. (At 1.30 in the morning! Why did no-one hear him? My office diary tells me I was in Leeds on that day and Alison would have been away at university, but why didn't Betty wake? He would have made quite a thump. It was all very peculiar but not important. I doubted – and still do – that he would have invented the episode. After all, he only confided it to his diary.) Those jottings, I realise reading them anew today and with a less emotional approach, do show signs of an incipient talent for writing. He was not afraid to express himself, in prose and verse, in a idiosyncratic and quite undisciplined way. He was writing only for himself and at the age of seventeen, but, even at that early age, he showed inventiveness and originality. Later, much later, we had proof of his lively mind and hunger for experience. On his last Christmas in 1978 he confided to his sister that he had been struck with curiosity and compassion for the dossers sleeping out rough in the bitter cold of that December in the city that housed the university. So he decided to join them temporarily and spent one freezing night curled up in a doorway in the centre of the city "to see what it was like." Even the most indulgent father can perhaps be excused for thinking that Paul would have made a most interesting and maybe unusual adult had he lived.

Back in that dark Spring and Summer of 1979, I waded through the course books that my son had studied. More about them later, but I emerged from them, blinking and still more worried about the nature of the course. I began reading a little more widely about suicide and also began talking – albeit with great caution – to people with some sort of experience in the field who might help me to sort out my thinking.

One dear friend emerged who was of great practical help. She herself had a close, personal brush with suicide as a young student and, having gained her M.A. in English was now teaching English literature at a college of further education. More to the point, she was an old friend of the man who, at the time of Paul's death, was a leading member of the staff of his university and very much involved in setting courses. She volunteered to go and see him with the intention of putting my case for an end to the course and backing it up with her own research from reading a wide range of experts on the subject. At that time, I did not realise the sacrifice she was making, for the man had been involved with her many years before and she far from relished seeing him again. But, showing the care and love that was so much part of her character, she put aside her fears and undertook the journey. (I do not give her name now. I have long since lost touch with her and would not wish to bring her identity, perhaps against her will, into these very personal remembrances).

On her return from the university she gave me a copy of the notes she took of the interview. They summarised the points she made and the response they provoked. At the end, she summed up the meeting like this: "I met a solid wall of resistance to all my arguments... I am ashamed to tell you the truth, to know someone whom I think so seriously lacks compassion and understanding. And I don't say that because I was resentful at feeling defeated, but because I think he was determined not to waver in any way from the fixed ideas he had before I arrived to talk to him."

My feelings at this point were ambiguous. Both Betty and I retained a great sense of gratitude for the way in which the authorities – and the students – at Paul's college had rallied round to search for him and the extreme solicitude with which they had treated us, even to the point of identifying his body to spare us this agony. Yet my mind was now beginning to harden against what I perceived to be their intransigent stand in defending this "Absurd" course. Oh, I understood their fundamental point that works of established literary value – however contentious the subjects and the opinions expressed – had to be introduced and taught to youngsters studying for a degree in English. Nevertheless, I grew increasingly to feel that their resistance to changing the course was a Pavlovian reaction to outside interference, a display of intellectual arrogance that was allowing an effete, ivory-towered snobbism to override consideration for human emotions and even lives.

(Betty concurred with this view but it is only fair to say that Alison did not. She empathised with the college's decision that, despite the risks involved, it should continue to encourage their students to stretch their minds and examine life's darker aspects through the writings of authors of international reputation. Then, as now, we agreed to disagree on this important point.)

I simmered for a while and returned to my reading. I devoured the then standard work, A. Alvarez's "The Savage God – A Study of Suicide," and dipped into relevant works by Kafka and Durkheim (prompted by my so much better educated friend), before settling down to read the two works by Camus that sat so prominently in the centre of this controversy.

I found myself puzzled by them. I was disturbed on two counts. Firstly, I could not understand why they carried the status of "classics" – particularly in the case of the novel, "The Outsider." Secondly, I could not comprehend why the second book, a collection of six essays entitled "The Myth of Sysiphus," the lead essay of which – a deeply philosophical, forty thousand word study of suicide – was a main element in a first year course for English undergraduates.

The two works have sat on my bookshelf for thirty years, yellowing now in their distinctive Penguin paperback covers. I took them down and began re-reading them for the purpose of this book. "Modern Classics," indeed – it says so on their covers. Perhaps, in those highly charged days of 1979, I had misjudged them. Then, I had certainly built up a head of hate-filled steam for Albert Camus and the influence that he had obviously exerted on my son and I was probably in no condition to read these works as objective contributions to the literature of suicide. My grey hairs of 2009, however, might give me a different perspective.

They did not.

Albert Camus was only 29 when he wrote "L'Etranger" (The Outsider) in 1942, the same year that he published "Le Mythe de Sisyphe." Born and brought up in North Africa, he had many jobs, including keeping goal for the Algerian national football team, before he came to Metropolitan France and became a journalist. During the war he was active in the resistance and became editor of the underground newspaper "Combat". He wrote many other books, including "The Plague" and "The Rebel", and was awarded the Nobel Prize for Literature in 1957. He died in a road accident in January 1960.

A formidable figure, then. I read "The Outsider" first. In simple, stripped-down prose, it tells the story of a young clerk in Algiers who leads an empty, unemotional existence, observing life almost as an outsider, but who kills a young Arab on a beach, is arrested and charged with murder. The novel ends with the man awaiting the guillotine, laying open his heart "to the benign indifference of the universe." The last lines read, "all that remained was to hope that on the day of my execution there should be a huge crowd of spectators and that they should greet me with howls of execration."

Told in the first person only, rarely does the story reveal any deep emotion within the mind of Mersault, the "hero" or give rational reasons for his acts. In fact, Mersault seems to have nothing on his mind at all. It appears to be an empty vessel. It is difficult to infer the reason for looking for the Arab on the beach and then shooting him dead. There had been a trite altercation between the man and one of Mersault's acquaintances – he didn't seem to acquire friends – and there is reference to the sun beating down and the heat becoming intolerable. But that is all. A nihilistic nothingness, an "absurd" nothingness, if you like – presumably reflecting the basic absurdity of all existence – pervades the slim story.

Camus was a friend of Jean Paul Sartre, who wrote of the book: "The Outsider is not at all a morbid book, it is a violent affirmation of health and sanity... He" (the hero) "is a classical Mediterranean. I would call his pessimism "solar" if you remember how much black there is in the sun. The philosophy of Camus is a philosophy of the absurd and for him the absurd springs from the relation of man to the world, of his legitimate aspirations to the vanity and futility of human wishes. The conclusions which he draws from it are those of classical pessimism."

Back in 1979, I had scrawled "classical pessimism be buggered" by the side of these words. But it was more important for me to look again at Paul's own sidelining throughout the book.

He had marked some of Camus's more felicitous descriptions in what one must presume to be approval, viz, "I knew I'd shattered the balance of the day." But he also sidelined some solitary and rather chilling phrases: "robot-like gestures," "all that was pretty futile" and "I've often thought that if I had been compelled to live in the trunk of a dead tree, with nothing to do but gaze up at the patch of sky just overhead, I'd have got used to it by degrees..." Further on: "I had stopped thinking altogether," and "it wasn't despair I felt but fear."

On my first reading, I had been looking forensically for evidence that Camus's musings had fuelled Paul's depression. Now, I disciplined myself to be more objective, remembering that the boy was studying both books, of course, for the purpose of writing essays on them. As a student, therefore, he would be looking for phrases and arguments that summed up Camus's arguments about the absurd.

What were those arguments?

The blurb on the cover of "Myth" calls the book "one of the clearest and strongest philosophical statements written about our time and ranks with its author's most important work. In it he asks the most difficult of all questions – why man, sensing the absurdity of his existence and unable to come to terms with the universe, does not commit suicide? Camus answers with a moving acceptance of the human condition on its proper terms, revolt, liberty and passion."

Er... yes. Camus himself, writing in his preface to the English edition of the work in 1953, has perhaps a better stab at it. "The fundamental subject... is this: it is legitimate and necessary to wonder whether life has a meaning, therefore it is legitimate to meet the problem of suicide face to face. The answer, underlying and appearing through the paradoxes which cover it, is this: even if one does not believe in God, suicide is not legitimate. Written fifteen years ago, in 1940, amidst the French and European disaster, this book declares that even within the limits of nihilism it is possible to find the means to proceed beyond nihilism... Although The Myth of Sisyphus poses mortal problems, it sums itself up for me as a lucid invitation to live and to create, in the very midst of the desert."

An argument against suicide, then? No. "The Outsider" is not that. It is a flat, arid novel about a completely uninteresting young man who commits a tragic and seemingly irrational act. There is nothing in the writing to give the story charm, force or reason and, given the same material, Conrad would have made the story come alive. Even considered as an intellectual tract, it remains obscure, at least to this reader. "The Myth" is a different matter. This is philosophy at the most arcane level, which sets out to address the question of The Absurd and suicide in metaphysical, Platonistic terms. As an argument against suicide, it is abstruse and highly discursive. In "The Outsider," Camus writes with economy. Here he is effulgent. The Fog Index is high and the target readership would seem to be mature students working on a doctorate.

One example of the prose: "Dying voluntarily implies that you have recognised, even instinctively, the ridiculousness characterised by that habit (of making the gestures commanded by existence for many reasons), the absence of any profound reason for living, the insane character of that daily agitation and the uselessness of suffering."

One would hope that Camus would make the concluding paragraph of the book a clear summation of what had gone before, some kind of valedictory coda to leave the reader nodding in agreement and approval. But this is what he writes:

"All that remains is a fate whose outcome alone is fatal. Outside of that single fatality of death, everything, joy or happiness, is liberty. A world remains of which man is the sole master. What bound him was the illusion of another world. The outcome of his thought, ceasing to be renunciatory, flowers in images. It frolics – in myths, to be sure – but myths with no other depth than that of human suffering and like it, inexhaustible. Not the divine fable that amuses and blinds, but the terrestrial face, gesture and drama in which are summed up a difficult wisdom and an ephemeral passion."

Unfair, of course, to quote out of context and, perhaps, both books may have suffered in translation (although they have different translators and it would have been an unlucky author indeed who was handicapped this way in consecutive publications). Nevertheless, the reader must throw up his hands and think of pots calling the kettle black when Camus writes of the works of Heidegger, Jaspers, Chestov and Husser: "If one could say just once, 'this is clear,' all would be saved. But these men view with one another in proclaiming that nothing is clear, all is chaos, that all man has is his lucidity and his definite knowledge of the walls surrounding him."

It would certainly help if, in either of the books, Camus could have explained why the world is absurd. His implication is that, because no-one outside the ranks of the religious can explain the meaning of life – why the hell we are here – then the whole experience is absurd. I would argue that for most of us, absurd is not the word at all. We may be happy or unhappy, questing or complacent, but to most of us, the world is there to be experienced for what it is: green and arid, full of happiness and unhappiness, a fascinating lottery that is to be got on with, and improved by self effort. Absurd? No. Intriguing? Definitely.

This non-intellectual, perhaps commonplace view is not given a moment's consideration in either of these so influential books. It makes me wonder what kind of goalkeeper Camus was. Did he sit down the night before a match and, using ruler and compass, work out the angles that the opposing strikers would use to come at him and then plot his own movements to counter them? I would love him better if he was just an instinctive shot-stopper.

Yet, from the evidence of his tutor, Paul accepted Camus's convoluted arguments against suicide and, indeed, presented a reasonably cogent case supporting the author's view when the books were debated in seminar. Perhaps those sidelinings he had made against the text were, indeed, merely his notes for the analyses of the works that were demanded by the course, an aide-memoir for the essay he was to write. I am sure that that is how it started. Yet most of the marks emphasise the many bleak negatives that Camus deploys in his arguments. One in particular struck at my heart.

It comes from a later essay in Myth, titled "Summer in Algiers," one not set for study. Paul's pencil had underlined this passage: "Men find here throughout all their youth a way of living commensurate with their beauty. After that, decay and oblivion. They've staked all on the body and they know that they must lose. In Algiers, for those who are young and alive, everything in their haven and all occasions for excelling – the bay, the sun, the red and white checkerboard of terraces going down to the sea, the flowers and stadiums, the fresh brown bodies... But for those whose youth is past no place exists, no sanctuary to absorb their melancholy."

What a great message of hope for later life! What decadent, all-embracing rubbish!

When I embarked on re-reading these "classics" I did so with the worry that, all those years ago, I may have been rather unfair to the university when, after much thought, I had written to the Master of Paul's College making what I had hoped was a measured case against them continuing the course on "The Absurd." Now, I have no such doubts and would write the same letter again.

This is what I wrote on 21st August 1979, although I have now deleted the names of those concerned:

Please forgive me for bothering you and returning to the painful subject of the death of my son, Paul. I have now had an opportunity of reflecting, more tranquilly, on the circumstances surrounding his suicide and I would like to put some thoughts to you and to ask your advice.

My concern mainly lies in the course entitled "The Absurd," which you may remember Paul had just begun. I appreciate that the subject matter of the course is not your responsibility but, short of writing to the Vice Chancellor, I am unsure about whom to approach at the university and I am therefore taking advantage of the sympathy you have already displayed towards us.

I understand that the university is continuing to offer, without modifications, the "Absurd" course to first year students. I have strong doubts about the wisdom of this, now that I have read the two books that were Paul's introduction to the course (Albert Camus's "The Outsider" and "The Myth of Sisyphus"), have studied the depositions that were submitted by the university at the inquest and talked at length to friends who are teachers or lecturers and others who are social workers.

When my wife, my daughter and I visited... shortly after Paul was found, we discussed the course — albeit superficially — with Dr A and two of his colleagues. Without in any way conceding that the course had contributed to Paul's death, Dr A did intimate, at the end of our talk on that day, that he felt that "The Absurd" might be discontinued or altered in some way for future academic sessions in the light of the experience of Paul's death.

At the inquest, however, Mr B robustly rejected the Coroner's suggestion that it was strong meat for such young minds and he stated that it was impossible to change the course in any way and still retain it as a viable part of the curriculum for students of English and American literature. I believe he also stated (my memory is a little hazy on this point and I am still awaiting from the Coroner the transcript of the inquest proceedings) that it was equally impracticable to improve the pastoral services of the university to make easier the detection of a potential suicide. At the end of a long cross examination of the university's witnesses, the Coroner concluded the dialogue with these words: "I have no doubt that those in charge will have due regard for what they have heard in court today. They should know that suicide is a very real and deep matter which affects the mind and that these forms of lectures should be kept in a buoyant manner so that death is not mocked. It is very real." (The source here is my own verbatim shorthand note.)

Mr B's view that no changes could or should be made were upheld some six weeks later when a friend of mine, Miss Y, who is herself an ex-university lecturer in English literature and who now teaches the subject at a college of further education, journeyed to the college to discuss Paul's death with Mr X, who I believe is the current... I should explain that Miss Y is an old friend of Mr X.

Mr X argued that, although the subject matter of the course may well have been the catalyst for Paul's suicide, it was precisely because the ideas in "The Absurd" were important and powerful that they must be put forward to university students. A university, he went on, could not be held responsible if the ideas it represented were acted upon. If so, its staff could be held responsible if, for example, their courses on urban guerrilla warfare produced terrorists. In other words, Paul's death was tragic but unpredictable. He felt that it was not necessary as a result of it to consider altering the course itself; nor offering it to a different, older group of students; nor monitoring their reactions.

At this point, you must be wondering what I am getting at. And, particularly, you may well refer to the note I wrote to you about Paul for his friends two weeks after his death, a copy of which I sent to you. Even more specifically, you may recall a passage in it which read as follows:

'But there is no question in our minds that his sensitive brain having been pushed too far by this work, nor do we attach any blame at all to the university staff...'

I confess that if I were to write that note now, having attended the inquest and having read some of the set books for the course, I would change it somewhat. I hasten to add that my family and I still attach no blame to the university staff. We have no bitterness to anyone at the university and we remember with painful gratitude the care of Dr A, yourself and others during the nightmare week-end when the search for Paul was raised. This is no witch-hunt but a sincere attempt to probe the factors leading to his death so that lessons can be learned and the chances of a tragic repetition reduced.

In this context, then, can any of us now believe that "The Absurd" course was not a contributory factor to his suicide? I have no doubt now that it played a part – perhaps a large part – in convincing him that life was not worth living; that, perhaps, it was well, absurd.

If this is so and the university has decided that the course needs no amendment, nor extra surveillance; that Paul's death was, if you like, an unfortunate but inevitable price that has to be paid if minds are to be extended; then I am deeply disappointed. Indeed, on the evidence I have so far, I am not sure that the Coroner's hope that "those in charge will have due regard for what they have heard in Court today" was well founded.

Let me try and be a little more constructive, although this is difficult because I am not an educationalist.

I have four main worries about the course and Paul's end.

1. Is "The Absurd" fundamental to a degree in English? Is it necessary to group together into one term's work (the main work of the term, indeed, to those who choose it) such a daunting, esoteric and macabre body of reading? The deposition to the inquest court states, of the course, "We shall seek to determine how far the Absurd originates in the dissolution of certain frames of reference… and to what extend their erosion alters our notion of the human being." The authors of the course are, I am sure, aware that Durkheim, the acknowledged authority on the sociology of suicide, states that when the structure of ideas on which a society is based appears to be crumbling or is in doubt, then the suicide rate increases. I would have thought that first year students were particularly vulnerable to a bit of crumbling. Nor does the fact that it is a popular course now impress me, in retrospect. All of us, in particular late teenagers, have a fascination with death. It is not unhealthy if treated in a balanced way, but this course savours to me of – no morbid pun intended – operation overkill. A good term's study of hard-core pornography might be less lethal. And it would probably be even more popular! All in all, I cannot reconcile the course's place in the curriculum. Its emphasis is on philosophy, i.e. on ideas and truths, rather than on the literary treatment of life and death ("the emphasis at all times will be on issues and ideas rather than literary criticism" – the deposition). Mr B in his deposition, wrote that "The Absurd" was "an essentially academic course." I am not sure what that means but I believe that the ideas presented in the first part of the course did not prove to be merely academic to my son. And, anyway, if ideas seem important and true, they will form the basis of actions of brave and sensitive people. Indeed, Camus says in the opening pages of "The Myth of Sysiphus", "For a man who does not cheat, what he believes to be true must determine his action." The appeal to young people in particular of consistency and integrity must be very great. Teachers surely know this. We are all responsible for each other and this respect must lie especially heavily on teachers.

2. This point of balance. If there has to be a course on The Absurd, does it have to start off so heavily, with Camus and Kafka? Could not the Monty Python referred to in the

deposition creep in earlier, to provide leavening? I can't help feeling that my son's sense of humour might just have saved him, if it could have been engaged. There appears precious little to laugh at in Camus.

3. If, as I hope is not the case, The Absurd survives this polemic, can it not be offered instead to third year students, or, even better, as a post-graduate course? I do suggest that undergraduates of 18–19 years of age are a particularly vulnerable group to be exposed to these highly sophisticated musings on death and suicide. It is nonsense to argue that it is not possible to judge at what age students are mature enough to handle difficult ideas. These judgments are made every day by teachers and principals in all kinds of educational establishments. I believe it to be a fair rule of thumb to presume that the older the student, the more mature and capable is his mind.

4. In a university the size of yours, I can well understand the problems of administering any kind of pastoral care. I am still puzzled that a comparatively gregarious student like Paul could hang himself on Tuesday and the alarm only be given on Saturday (this, too, after he had spoken to his flatmate of suicide on the previous Sunday) but this kind of retrospection is arid and I am now concerned with the future. Obviously the university staff cannot be full time shepherds and you must rely, most of the time, on students to pick up incipient suicidal tendencies in their fellows. Equally obviously, it would be wrong to over emphasise these dangers to the undergraduates. But is it not possible to alert in particular those who are embarking on course, such as The Absurd, which do deal with suicide? There may be better ways of handling the danger and you would know them. But I find it difficult to believe that, after Paul's death, nothing has been, nor will be, changed.

I feel that that is enough to be going on with. Again, I do apologise not only for the length of this letter but for addressing it to you. Perhaps it is a matter for the Vice Chancellor. May I impose on you to see that it reaches the right quarters? As you can see, I am concerned about the matter and am anxious to do all I can to try and ensure that no other parent of one of your undergraduates suffers the anguish that my wife and I have known since May 1st.

Thank you.

To my shame, in the intervening thirty years I have somehow lost the reply that this blast evoked. However, I do remember that my arguments and requests were met with the straightest of straight bats. The reply was sympathetic but it did not give an inch nor stray from the principles expressed in the deposition at the inquest nor given to me orally afterwards.

However, tucked away at the bottom of the letter there was a simple paragraph – almost a postscript – saying that I would be interested to know that The Absurd course had been dropped for the coming term. There was, it seemed, little interest displayed in it by the students...

I felt no sense of triumph. Just a renewal of sadness, for if it was a victory it was a pyrrhic one, gained at the cost of Paul's death. I also experienced – and still do – a suppressed fury at those rafts of famous philosophers and, yes, perhaps some of the teachers at university, who see the great sociological problem of suicide as a fascinating subject to be probed and dissected on a public platform erected on academic scaffolding. Of course, self-destruction is a matter for the mind, but it should also engage the emotions, for it is dangerous material. It kills, you know. (In this context, I felt a shaft of gratitude fly from me to Alvarez when I read in "The Savage God" his belief that the Samaritans, who set up their first emergency centre in 1953, do more in a month to prevent suicide than scientists manage in a decade.)

Yes, Paul agreed with Camus that suicide was wrong (although how he got through the Algerian's psychobabble and bad writing to reach this point I shall never know). But he still went out, in the middle of reading "The Outsider" and hanged himself. I believe that Camus's sinuous arguments played a role in making up his mind. They showed him that suicide was not unthinkable. It was a rational act that could by analysed and dignified by intellectual gobbledegook and made almost respectable – a way of resolving and escaping from the pain of life.

Camus should have stayed between his goalposts.

But is this The Why of It? Should I blame Camus and the other earnest academics for Paul's death? At the time – or, at least, four months or so after it, when I had pondered on it for that time – I more-or-less did so. Yet, even then, I felt uneasy about this conclusion. It was far too facile. The bleak writings of Camus may indeed have been the final element that pushed our son over the edge but he had obviously been depressed when entering into the great philosophical debate. Depressed over what, then? It was true that, rather surprisingly for a sociable boy, he seemed not to have made good new friends at college and was missing those he had left behind at his school. But there was no great failed love affair, no bouts of drinking, no drug taking and, to repeat, he was handling his work well. I read now that a predeliction towards suicide can be genetic. Was there a previous act of self destruction in the family? Yes, well, sort of. My sister tells me that our grandmother's brother-in-law had cut his throat (indeed, our mother as a child had helped grandmother to "lay him out" – another contributory factor to making those brown eyes always so soulful). But he was not of our blood and surely the atavistic gap was too great to leap anyway. No clue there, nor anywhere, it seemed.

I had stressed in that early article that to us all Paul was an ordinary child, except in the leadership qualities that he had shown as a boy and teenager and in his proficiency at games, his cheerfulness and his undoubted popularity with teachers and his peers. In doing so, I guess I was anxious to dispel any doubts that he was some sort of secret manic depressive, which we all agreed he was not. Yet the references made to his playing truant on one occasion while he sat for two days and thought in a park; his solitary, early morning adventure on the stairs; and him evincing signs of self-doubt to his mother on a visit home just before Christmas, were not the only signs of a departure from the ordinary that he displayed in the months leading up to his death.

On Sunday 2nd July 1978, we held our silver wedding anniversary party in the garden of our house in Kingswood, Surrey. Family and old and new friends gathered and the sun shone. Paul had returned from Paris for the occasion a few days before, seemingly happy to be home and with his great wrap-around grin much in evidence. He immediately looked up his old friends in the neighbourhood and had a couple of nights out with them immediately before the weekend.

On the second occasion he borrowed Betty's car, a small Ford Escort, and did not reappear until the small hours. The car, he said, had been stolen and he did not know where it was. The next day, his mother heard that he had been seen driving the car "like a madman" round and round the path fronting the main building in the grounds of his old school, a girl at his side, until, eventually, he had crashed it, writing it off. The wreck had been found, of course, and traced to Betty. She confronted Paul who stoically denied the story for several hours, until finally confessing.

This was all most upsetting, of course. The loss of the car hardly mattered but Paul's behaviour did. It was so uncharacteristic that it was worrying, for he had always been an honest boy and we had never seen him drunk. In the end he said that he was merely "having a bit of fun" and that the car had got out of control. I stayed out of it all, not wishing to have a heavy scene on the eve of our celebration, but it did cast a cloud for us over our party and Paul was suitably chagrined, even morose, through it. Then he recovered and went back to Paris, the grin much in evidence again.

We put these strange deviations down to the ups and downs of being a teenager, parts of the rites of passage in growing up. The term bipolar disorder was not about then, or, at least if it was, the Wilcox family, despite its desperate searching for a reason, had not heard of it. It was our daughter, Alison, who first mentioned it to me, when she learned that I was contemplating writing about Paul at last. I have now dug into the subject as best my determinedly unscientific brain would allow.

It seems clear that the illness is not a single disorder but a category of mind disarrangements in which periods of an abnormally elevated mood and boundless energy are interspersed with what can be severe depressive phases. According to the US Government's Institute of Mental Health there is no single cause for bipolar disorder, whatever its category, but late adolescence and early adulthood are peak years for the onset of the condition. Although the disorder affects people differently, individuals with the illness tend to be much more outgoing and daring than "normal" people and there is evidence to suggest that the disorder is found in large numbers of youngsters who are creative and go on to work in the arts. And it can lead to suicide.

Dr Thomas Joiner, Bright-Burton Professor of Psychology at Florida State University, earned from me an additional quota of respect when I read his book "Why People Die of Suicide" (Harvard University Press, Cambridge Mass., 2005), in that his heart as well as his brain had become immersed in the study of suicide. His own father had become a victim of bipolar disorder and taken his life. Dr Joiner, then, had been there personally as well as studied it.

It is impossible to sum up such a learned work in a few words – and I don't want this account to become bogged down with technical analyses of the causes of suicide – but his main conclusion seemed to ring true to me. He writes that people are not born with the developed capacity to seriously injure themselves. In fact, they are usually born with the opposite: the knee-jerk reaction to avoid pain, injury and death. Evolution has seen that we have strong tendencies towards self-preservation. But these can be overcome if certain conditions apply, namely if the would-be suicide feels real disconnection from others and that he feels ineffective to the point of seeing himself as being a burden to others. So: thwarted belongingness and perceived burdensomeness, often resulting from bipolar disorder. In a welter of statistics scattered through his book, Dr Joiner notes that May is the favourite month for suicides of those suffering from the disorder.

Ah! It all fitted: the creativity displayed in Paul's poetry and other writings, his good schoolwork and in leading the discussion on Camus; the daring he showed in hurling himself down the stairs (I think, head first); his outgoing nature as evinced by his wide circle of chums and succession of girlfriends; the strange ups and downs shown by the reclusive escape to that park for two days, the falling into the Seine and, of course, the strange episode of the car crash.

What didn't quite jell was the "thwarted belongingness and perceived burdensomeness" reference. Paul grew up in a loving and liberal home and, as far as we could, we never imposed burdens on him. We had agreed without demur when he asked to leave his Oxbridge class at school and go to a provincial university, although this was a disappointment to us and to his teachers, who felt that he would easily pass the entrance examination. Yet who was to know the problems, real and imagined, that obviously pressed so heavily on him in those last few months? He was far from home and friends and even, perhaps, feeling a bit of a failure (not going to Oxford, wrecking the car). Nonsense in reality, of course, but a strong possibility as a source of his undoubted depression.

Trying to make a diagnosis thirty years after the event is ridiculous, of course, but bipolar disorder of some kind or other seems to be as near as any of us can get to discovering the Why of It. The effect of his brutal death on our small family (there are now just three of us, in that our daughter is now divorced and has been unable to have children, which means, of course, that Betty and I have no grandchildren) has been in no way divisive. In our search for some rational reason for Paul's rejection of us – for that is what suicide always appears to those left behind – we had never even thought of blaming each other. In fact, our son's departure has driven the three of us much closer together, in a self-supporting, warm relationship. Given the passage of time and the strong desire to let sleeping loved ones lie, we all agree that we must now leave it at that. But, back in 1981, two years after his death, Paul himself was not quite prepared to leave it there and we must, then, put the clock back again to that time.

Chapter 15

THE END OF IT

One rather bleak Sunday afternoon in February, a little under two years after Paul's death, Betty and I were sitting in the drawing room of our house in Islington, watching the film "Khartoum" and desperately trying to believe in the 6ft 4in Charlton Heston as the 5ft 3in General Charles Gordon. We were about to give up the struggle when Alison and her old school friend and former neighbour, Barbara, came through the door and asked us to switch off the film, because they had "something important" to say. What ensued changed our lives once again.

Barbara was visiting with us from Australia and had been sleeping in Paul's old room. We knew from the days when she was growing up next door to us in Epsom, Surrey, that she was alleged to have psychic powers, even as a girl – perhaps especially as a little girl. She had, it seemed, always been accompanied by some sort of spiritual companion, whom she called "Auntie," who went with her everywhere and whom she took completely for granted. I, at least, rather took these claims with a shovelful of snuff, but the girl never made a fuss about it and in every other way was completely conventional, so that it never became an issue.

It was Alison, however, who now began relating the strange happenings in our house that had involved both of the girls in the last few days. Our daughter explained that, two evenings ago, she had been sitting in her bedroom with Barbara when she gradually became aware of what seemed like an increase in the barometric pressure in the room. It was, she said as though some giant extractor was sucking all of the air out the room. The atmosphere became oppressive, "close and crowded." She did not feel any presence of evil at all but she was frightened because she could not understand what was happening. Barbara, however, who was also in the room, seemed unperturbed and, when Betty called the girls to dinner, Alison decided to say nothing about the incident, presuming that a change in the weather had caused the feeling.

The next day, however, Barbara confessed to her friend that she, too, had experienced the strange oppression in the room. Barbara then took up her telling of the story to us.

For several days previously, she said, she had been aware of Paul's presence as she sat in his old bedroom. He never materialised visually but she knew he was there and, as the hours went by, her awareness of him grew stronger and his presence more oppressive. It was unmistakeably Paul, whom she remembered, of course, from her childhood, and his weight became heavier, so that she felt she had a permanent headache. She pleaded with him to go away but he persisted. It had all peaked on the evening when she sat with Alison. Although she betrayed no sign of this to her friend, she became, she said, almost overwhelmed by "a tremendous force," to the point where she almost blacked out. She realised that Paul was communicating to her his immense frustration and distress that he could not communicate with his sister and he was begging her to help him get through to her. He was terribly tired and emotional. She told him (unspokenly, in her mind) that she lacked the powers to link them but that she would try and find someone who could help. Immediately, he had left and the pressure had disappeared. Alison was unaware of this, except that she, too of course, had experienced the pressure.

The next day, Barbara suggested that they both visit the British Spiritualist Association where they might be able to find a medium who could help. Initially reluctant, Alison had eventually agreed and early that Sunday afternoon as we sat watching the beginning of the movie, they had boarded a bus to the Association's headquarters in Belgrave Square. There, Barbara had stayed outside while her friend filed into the big, rather gloomy building and drew a numbered ticket to take "pot luck" with one of the visiting mediums. He turned to be a heavily built, elderly, red-faced man from Lancashire named Arthur Ball. What ensued, told to us now in Alison's words, made us lose whatever fragment of interest we still retained in the Nile and the plight of General Gordon.

In a small room, in a one-to-one informal chat with Mr Ball, Paul had "come through" via the medium and in a tearful state of huge relief had assured her that he was "still alive" and loved her and us all. I don't intend to relate all that ensued in the next twenty five minutes or so because, since then, I have made it a rule only to present my own, first person account of these remarkable events. I do this because it is easy to discount experiences when related at third hand, when the temptations to embroider someone else's story to make it sound better are so real. Let me, however, relax that rule just to relate one incident. At the end of the session, Mr Ball asked Paul to give his sister "a sign" later, if he could, outside the conduit of the medium, to show her that it had not been some sort of fluke or fabrication. He explained that it had been extremely difficult for Paul to communicate – hence the boy's frustration, fatigue and high emotion – and that there would be no guarantee that her brother would succeed. He also did not know what the sign would be except that it would not be frightening. Merely some sort of personal, seemingly inexplicable, happening. Some time after her visit to Belgrave Square, Alison was brushing her hair in her bedroom before turning in. Barbara had returned to Australia and two other friends were staying in Paul's old room. Suddenly, Alison heard a kind of rumbling. She felt that it was strange, because she had never heard the sound of distant trains before and we lived miles from a station. Then her eye caught the photograph of Paul on her dressing table. It was rocking from side to side about one inch above the table, with its edges knocking the surface, as though an unseen hand was moving it. The dressing table contained many other photographs and items of memorabilia but everything else remained perfectly still. It was, of course, Paul's "sign," given at a time when, with others next door, it would not frighten her.

Alison's story of her meeting with Arthur Ball (for that's what it was, a straightforward meeting, there was no holding of hands, dimming of lights or other spiritualistic trappings) left us amazed, perplexed (in my case) and half-joyful (in Betty's). At the beginning Alison had warned me that I wouldn't necessarily believe or like what she was about to relate, for she knew that I had little belief in life after death and even less in contact with the spirit world. In fact, this was not quite true, for I was beginning to be impressed with recent cases of "after death" experiences I had read and, although my agnosticism and impatience with formal religion had grown stronger over the years, I endeavoured to keep an open mind on the question of "what next?" Having said that, both Betty and I, each in our own unspoken way, had pleaded for two years with our son to give us some sort of sign to ease our anguish. Nothing had resulted, of course. Until now.

What to do? It was agreed that Betty and I, separately and at an interval, would journey to the Society to see if we could reproduce Alison's experience. Alison suggested, however, that it would be better to see Arthur Ball, if possible. He had explained to her that communication with those "who had gone before" was extremely difficult. He gave the analogy that it was like trying to speak on the telephone to someone in Australia, via a bad connection with an interpreter in China. It helped to use the same "interpreter" (medium). He came down from Lancashire, it seemed, only occasionally to take his place on the Belgrave Square rota and it helped to make an appointment. He was never told the names of the people he was going to see. They came into his gloomy little room only as numbers on a ticket.

Betty resolved to go first. She was unable to see Mr Ball and her experience with a woman medium was less than satisfactory. Three weeks later Alison was able to see Arthur Ball again, with much the same heart warming results.

My turn came at last and on 14th May I met Arthur Ball. I was apprehensive – as much about the possibility of nothing happening as the thought of somehow "meeting" my son again. I was determined to remain unemotional and as objective as possible and I took along with me a new Biro pen and shorthand notebook. I asked Mr Ball if he minded if I took a note and he was quite unconcerned about that. He was as I expected: grizzled grey hair, thick set, with red jowls and speaking in the flat cadences of the north. His manner was matter-of-fact and conversational. It was like talking to a street corner grocer about the price of cabbage.

I deliberately did not give my name when we shook hands and nor did he ask it; I was merely number 7 on the red ticket. He enquired if I had visited the Association before and when I answered negatively he explained that there was no guarantee that we would have a successful session. Then the conversation took a farcical turn.

He asked if I had ever had anything to do with Ealing. Puzzled (what the hell did this have to do with Paul?) I thought for a moment and answered that I had an old chum who lived there but didn't know much about the place.

"No, no," he said. "Ealing. Ealing."

"Yes. The place in West London?"

"No. Ealing. Ealing."

This was ridiculous. And then I realised. Mr Ball, bless him, did not pronounce his aitches. He meant healing. "Sorry," I said in embarrassment. "Healing. No. No personal involvement at all."

He nodded. (And now I revert to my transcript of the verbatim shorthand note I took on that afternoon. What follows is an accurate reflection of the conversation. I have often been asked how I was able to continue to record what he said – there was rarely an interchange between us – even when I became emotional. I can only thank my training as a young reporter in many court rooms and council meetings, when it was quite possible to keep the pen flying over the paper while my mind was detached.) Mr Ball spoke in a stream of consciousness fashion, talking quite conversationally and often ungrammatically to me and to others in the room, although I could not see nor sense any other presence. He made no differentiation between talking to me and to others. It came out in one flow, but all in his own voice.

AB: *Have you made a study of spiritual feeling?*

JW: *Er… no.*

AB: *When we shook hands I felt it. This means a healer. Is your father over?*

JW: *Yes, he died a long time ago.*

AB: *He is in this room. If you ever get into a small group for meditation, you will find that your hands… the palms of your hands… will become very warm. I don't mean warm like today, because the weather's very warm. They come warm. That is the power of healing coming through you. If you begin to use it, I would ask you just to put it* (he held his hands up, palms towards me, and then demonstrated) *on your patients, on their shoulders, run down and when your hands stop then you will be inspired that something is wrong in that spot. And you will work in that way. The spirit friend that is giving this to you is a very beautiful North American Indian. He might be fifty. I note that he has two feathers at the back of his head. His hair is in a fringe and he has a headband. A very nice influence. He is talking about the power in both hands and that you can be useful to your fellow man. But use it when you feel you want to do it. Don't let anyone talk you into it not even me. Use it on your own initiative and on your own desires. Ask the Society here how to go about it. Did you ever want to be a doctor?*

JW: *No... well, I've always considered it as being the best and most honourable job in the world. But I knew that I was never clever enough.*

AB: *Well, you've got medicine within you and I feel that you can now bring it out by healing. You will be very pleased about it and very happy. Has your father been over long?*

(At this point I began to feel a little impatient. I had come here in the hope of communicating with my dead son. I didn't want to hear nonsense about Red Indians and my mystic healing powers, nor even to hear about my father, loved as he was. Where the hell was Paul?)

JW: *Yes. A long time.*

AB: *He is not an old man. He looks very young to me.* (He had died aged 52). *He is smiling. He is very happy. You have had your father given to you from the spirit world?*

JW: *No.*

AB: *He longs to see you. He has been longing to see you. Were you very close?*

JW: *No, because he died when I was only fourteen. But I always respected him very much. He was always ill. He was consumptive.*

AB: *There is a unity between your father and you now from the spirit world. And he is guiding you. Do you drive a car?*

JW: *Yes.*

AB: *He has been often in the car, but you wouldn't know his presence. And as he comes to see you... ah, he is trying to tell me that you must persevere as you are. Has there been a change with you?*

JW: *Er... yes.*

AB: *Yes, there is a change in atmosphere. Don't worry. It will come right in the end. You will be confused in the beginning but you see it always comes right in the end and he is guiding you in this matter. Can you* (speaking to Dad) *give him a sign? Yes.* (He brushes his right hand to the right side of his forehead.) *When you touch your head like this... only quickly... a second or so... your father is with you and that's your contact. If you will try and sit down, stop the car, and see what new thoughts – inspiration – comes into your mind, you will certainly be very happy to get these new inspirations with your life. He is very pleased. He says there is nothing wrong with me now. I am perfectly whole and I am all right. Will you let him know that I am often near. Is your mother in body?*

JW: *Yes.*

AB: *Have her circumstances changed?*

JW: *Well, yes. She hasn't married again. But she's moved around a bit.*

AB: *Yes. He couldn't quite keep up with her but he still loves her. He wants to thank you* (I could not quite hear Mr B's next sentence). *The time has come now when he wants you to study more about yourself and psychic matters and I feel that is the first thing to say to you.* (Short pause) *There is a grey light just come over you and I don't know what it is. Something about your health? Are you all right?*

JW: *Yes. I've got a bit of muscular trouble in my joints, that's all.*

AB: *It might be a depletion.*

JW: *What's that?*

AB: *You know – you are depleted. You are very sensitive. But do take care of yourself. Don't over-do it. There is mental tension. There is getting tense with you… I want you to be careful. Don't worry too much, it brings this tension on you.* (Short pause). *Have you got a son?*

JW: *No. He died two years ago.*

AB: *Was he very old?*

JW: *He was just twenty.*

AB: *Has he been back before?*

JW: *Yes, through you.*

AB: *Just a moment.* (He then seems to address me, but he is not, he is talking to someone else in the room.) *Oh, no, sorry. Don't cry. Yes, thank you. No, you don't know me, do you? Come along, don't cry. Yes, all right. I'll tell him.* (Mr B now coughs and, alarmingly, clutches his neck). *No. Don't remember your passing.* (To me) *He has got something around his neck.* (He grimaces and holds his neck again). *How did he die?*

JW: *He took his life. He hanged himself.*

AB: *Oh, I am sorry.* (Then, talking to Paul). *Don't get into that state. Keep calm. This is your Dad.* (Then to me) *He still loves you. I am sorry. I am very sorry. Yes I like your little moustache.* (Turning to me again). *I am trying to break him. That's better.* (To me). *You've got something on you that belongs to him… something around your neck. Your tie?* (I loosen my tie, unbutton my shirt and show Paul's ear ring that I had worn on a gold chain, hidden under my shirt, for the last eighteen months or so. I wear it to this day.) *Yes, a ring. He is talking about his sister. Talking about her cross. She is still wearing it. I love her. I didn't know… he didn't know that he would ever see you again. As soon as I began to see you… I know that I did wrong. I am very sorry, Dad, but I can't come back, only like this.* (Mr B now to Paul) *You can come any time.*

JW: *Tell him that we are not bitter and that we still love him.*

AB: *He knows that. He wants to… clear his conscience. Give my love to my Mom. I still love you all. I love you very much. He is pleased about someone – a lady who advised you to see a spiritualist about his life over there. He is thanking her very much. You will tell her, Dad, you will tell my sister to tell her. He is very happy. He is coming back to his natural self. He is talking about his little photograph again – have we seen it before? – oh: have you had a photograph enlarged or something?*

JW: *Yes.*

AB: *It is lovely. You have some flowers beside the photograph. He has seen it. He is thanking Mom for getting it done. Did you know your Dad was coming? Yes. I touched him when you were talking over it. Yes…* (to Paul) *they called me Mr Ball and talked about it? So my Dad decided to come. He is very happy to see you. You won't forget, Dad, to tell Mom and tell her that I love her. He is very fond of his mother's cooking. You don't get meat pies over here. Will you tell him that he was to come and see me again. I am coming home with you. Give my love to my sister. He is very fond of his sister. Tell her I still love her. She is lovely. Tell mother… Mom… about my photo. I love it. I am very pleased about it. And pleased about the flowers* (one word missed here in my shorthand note) *on Saturday. He picked his own flowers. I didn't know, Dad, how fond I was of you until now… and my mother.* (Mr Ball to Paul) *Don't cry. I love you all very much and I will always love you. There is one thing Dad. When you all come over — it might be a long time — we'll all meet again and be happy. Thank you very much.* (Mr Ball now in an aside to me) *I am sorry when they cry. Yes, you are very nice. He is doing that* (Mr Ball strokes an imaginary moustache) *to his little moustache. Do wear my ear ring, Dad, where you have got it. I picked it out. Your father* (mine) *has helped him the most.*

JW: *I thought it was my wife's mother* (Betty had said as much after an unsatisfactory session with another medium, of which more later).

AB: *Many people have helped him, he says. Grandma was first and I have learned how to get in touch with Grandad. Ah, I am sorry, but I am afraid we must leave it there. That is the end of our session.*

That is how it ended. Abruptly, as if a bell had rung, although I did not see Mr Ball even glance at his watch. Had Paul retreated, or was it merely that my half hour, or whatever it was (I can't remember now how long the entrance fee earned) had ended? It was a strange and even banal conclusion to an experience that had been hypnotic and very emotional for me. The shorthand note I have on my desk as I write this still shows the splashes where my tears fell even as I wrote.

Sniffling, I thanked Mr Ball and made my way out into the early spring sunshine in Belgrave Square and stood blowing my nose, while fumbling to put my notebook back into the briefcase I carried. I tried to think rationally.

There were several references that stirred the old scepticism within me. My "spirit friend." Why did these people always have to be Red Indians (remember Madame Arcati's spirit world contact in Coward's "Blithe Spirit?"). I felt uncomfortable with my father's urging me to "study psychic matters," which sounded all too much like Spiritualist Association propaganda, as was Mr Ball's reference to him "being whole again now." Then there was the rather hurried change by Mr B when he quoted Paul as saying that my father had helped him the most "on the other side" and I, puzzled, had said that Betty had reported Paul as saying that *her* mother had been his best aide: "Grandma was first and I had learned to get in touch with Grandad."

Then the session had been abruptly closed. Had my correction rather miffed Mr Ball? – perhaps the first intimation that I was a less than completely passive, uncritical listener?

Yet these cavils were far outweighed by the staggering detail that Paul had conveyed through Mr B – detail that Ball could not have known. In the two months before his death, Paul had grown a small moustache, which had been the subject of some mirth and (on Paul's side) some sensitivity. The matter had not arisen during Alison's visit and I, of course, had not brought it up during my meeting. Yet Ball/Paul referred to it. The cross that Alison wore had been Paul's present to her just before his death and, although hidden under a blouse, had been mentioned by Paul on her visit and then again when I arrived. Similarly, only Paul could have known that I was wearing his earring under my jacket, shirt and tie. And Paul's request that Barbara be thanked for her part in enabling him to communicate at last when I had not mentioned the girl at all… it all built up to an overwhelmingly powerful case that we had all, on our separate visits, indeed made contact with our son and brother.

One small, seemingly unimportant point niggled away at me as I stood staring unseeingly at the traffic circling the large island in Belgrave Square. Why should Mr Ball give me "a sign" from my father that involved brushing my forehead? Then it occurred to me. I had been fourteen when my father saw me for the last time. Then, I had long, rather lank hair that fell over my eyes and I was always brushing it away with my fingers. That is how he would have remembered me. Phew! It all fitted.

I started to walk to where my car was parked in the square on a meter. Then I remembered: did I not have healing powers that the Spiritualist Association would help me develop? It would be criminally wasteful to disregard this new talent. It was also all getting a bit too much, but I turned and made my way back to the reception desk anyway. The lady behind it was grey haired, blue sweatered and had a fierce, rather hooked nose. I tried to explain what Mr Ball had told me but she interrupted.

"Oh, many people have those powers," she sniffed. "It's not unusual at all. But it's difficult to develop them for use. In fact, I doubt if you will be able to. Here's a pamphlet you can read if you want to about courses you can take. Good afternoon."

I took the pamphlet and shuffled off. I never did pursue the matter. My career as a Great Healer was stillborn by Old Blue Sweater. Anyway, there were other, more momentous things to think about.

Back home in Islington, Betty, Alison and I compared notes. It was clear that Betty had suffered through not being able to see Arthur Ball and that it was important that she did so. She was lucky and four days after my own visit to Belgrave Square she was able to make her own pilgrimage and see the unassuming man from Lancashire. Thankfully, her experience was very similar to those of Alison and myself in that Paul "appeared" and spoke to her through Mr Ball. Again, I will not relate the details, except to record one particular incident. It seemed that some days before her appointment, Betty had gone on her own into our small garden in Islington, plucked a red rose and placed it before Paul's photograph in the bedroom. (Paul, of course, had referred to this on my visit to Mr B but I was unaware of it until then). Now, Paul had spoken of it again and told his mother how much the gesture had meant to him. Betty returned home to us, tearful, impressed and with her heart lifted for the first time since her son's death.

The three of us compared our experiences again and this time found them to be remarkably similar, although each session had contained small detail that was significant only to each of us individually. It all added up to a convincing body of evidence that there *was* life after death and that Paul, our much loved son and brother, was out there somewhere in some form or other. I still, perhaps, retained some remnants of doubt (the reference to meat pies "over here" and to us all meeting up to be together again one day, struck an over-sentimental chord to this old journalistic hack) but even so, I was convinced. The balm the experience brought to our questioning minds was like finding a cure for some dreaded disease. This was particularly true of Betty, whose mother's grief was the hardest to bear. She still carries that great sorrow of course, but I am convinced that it would have seemed an even heavier burden today without the meeting in Belgravia with that simple, greatly gifted, red-faced man from Lancashire who couldn't sound his aitches.

What to do next? Paul had asked us all to keep visiting him through Mr Ball, despite the effort and strain this seemed to cause him. We resolved that we would do so, although I feel that we all had some doubts about the propriety of it all. Somehow it didn't seem seemly to keep breaking through the barrier between the two worlds in an attempt "to speak" to Paul. Betty, for instance, had been told on her visit to Mr B that our son was "very busy" working with children in the other place and that he found this quite tiring. Should we attempt to keep plucking him back to exchange messages of love, given that we had all had those first, cathartic "meetings," that had done so much to put our minds at rest?

I decided to make one last visit but was unable to arrange a meeting with Mr B and, instead, had to endure half an hour of discomfort with a strange woman medium who kept throwing up strange people to me "from the other side" and making predictions for the future. No Paul this time. I felt I had been sitting in a caravan listening to a gypsy fortune teller.

Then, shortly afterwards, we heard that Arthur Ball had died, or, in his terminology, had "passed over." That decided the matter for us. We would let Paul rest in peace – or working hard with his spiritual children. We would not bother him again, but keep visiting him often and lovingly in our minds as our own lives moved onwards.

It was only some time afterwards that I suddenly realised that not one of us, in our encounters with Paul via Arthur Ball, had asked the obvious, burning question:

"Paul – why did you do it?" Perhaps it was some sort of feeling of impropriety that prevented us from grasping this nettle – literally, a case of intruding into private grief. Or was it, as with me, simply a matter of listening so hard to Ball's non-stop narrative that the opportunity somehow didn't seem to occur? Anyway, it is of no matter now.

Alvarez writes in "The Savage God" that no single theory will untangle an act as ambiguous and with such complex motives as suicide. He offers no solutions and doesn't believe that solutions exist, since suicide means different things for different people at different times. I now favour the theory that Paul did have a form of bipolar disorder, probably developed only shortly before his death, so that he had had no time to create a *modus operandi* for dealing with it, and we, of course, had similarly not been able to recognise it. If we had been able to ask Paul the question, then, through Arthur Ball, I guess he would only have been able to say, "sorry, but I was so depressed…"

Have I become a convinced spiritualist, in view of our experiences?

Well, yes and no. Despite our respect for the late Arthur Ball, I am uneasy with the structured part of the process of contacting the departed ones: the complete reliance on a medium and the dependence on he/she presenting – or perhaps interpreting? – the messages from "the other side." And I eschew the links, when they are offered, between life after death and conventional religion. I do not believe in heaven or hell and I cannot bring myself to make the intellectual leap that will allow me to believe in the existence of a God or in the claims of any of the messiahs that have trodden this earth so many years ago. I am with Darwin rather than the Book of Genesis.

Yet I cannot explain the many personal details about Paul and his death that Mr Ball revealed to us without reverting to the view that he, our son, is in existence, in some form or other, in a world beyond this one. Yes, of course it gives us comfort, and part of me remains a bit suspicious of that but, damn it all, I am weary of being a sceptic. I have always been rather jealous of the serene solace given to the religious by their unquestioning faith. I think the Wilcox family is due a little comfort and I believe it's fair to allow us to hug this to us.

However, I must confess to a subtle but important change that has occurred in my own thinking about Paul's suicide over the years.

In trying to analyse, back in 1979, the role I might have played in his death, I came to the conclusion that I could not feel personally guilty about it. I take a different view now. If the first duty of a government is to defend the State, then, similarly, the first duty of a parent must be to protect his children. Oh, I had assumed this responsibility diligently when Paul was a little boy. Although I hate heights, I followed him, holding onto his jersey, as the small figure climbed rocks and inched out onto high branches of trees. But I markedly did not do so as he grew up. Of course, I could not watch over him when, at the age of 20, he went to university, any more than I could have been his constant guardian when he was beginning to find his feet as a teen-aged young man. But, looking back now, I believe that I was tunnel-visioned through those years in that I devoted far too much time to my career and insufficient to my family when the children were growing up. I came home late during the week and, at weekends in the summer, cricket assumed a disproportionate importance to me. I was selfish and self-centred. When the time came when perhaps I might have made a difference, Paul could not confide in me. The gap that I had allowed to grow between us was too wide to leap.

I do not flagellate myself about this; there is no point, anyway. Nor do I feel that I am wallowing in self pity. But I do now recognise it and wish – oh how I wish! – that I could have had another go at this parenting business. It's only when it's too late that you begin to get the hang of it...!

The affect of the spiritualistic experience on Betty and Alison was marked. As I have already written, it lifted to some extent the terrible sadness that had descended on Betty and did, I feel, restore her religious faith. Now, in maturity, she has moments of great depression, particularly when she looks around at contemporaries enjoying their many grandchildren. But I am sure that these would have been more frequent and even more distressing had Paul not "broken through."

As for Alison, the experience was much more cathartic than her mother and I suspected at the time. She has recently shown me copies of two letters that she sent in the spring of 1981 to close friends living abroad. In pages of remarkably elegant and deeply felt prose for one so young, she refers to the depression she used to feel (which obviously created the morose face she presented to us as a child): "I am much, much happier and really do feel a genuine peace – a peace I've never really experienced before. I'm still me and I still get depressed; nothing, however, like the blackness that often used to come over me before – a blackness that had nothing to do with Paul's death incidentally. It had always been there..."

And in the second letter, referring to her "conversation" with her brother via Ball: "Paul has suffered all right, but *not* at the hands of some power who has judged him and meted out punishment of hell-fire. It has been his *own* conscience and his *own* judgement of himself that has been his Hell. He has seen us suffer and for two years he has been trying to get through to us. His relief at finally doing so was as strong as his determination had been. There was and is so much love... I have been greatly privileged and have gained something that I have never looked for and never tried to find out about..."

She has confirmed now that she still feels that way. And the old "blackness" has never returned.

Suicide has taken on a seemingly new guise as a weapon used by Muslim extremists who are promised countless virgins in paradise if they take Western unbelievers with them as they detonate the explosives strapped to their waists or laid in their cars. In fact, there is nothing new in this. The same promise was made by the

Mahdi to his Dervishes who flung themselves onto the bayonets of the British soldiers in Wolseley's abortive attempt to rescue General Gordon in the Sudan of 1885. But its longevity does nothing to give it respectability in warfare. It remains a morally disgusting – and militarily expensive – way of inflicting damage on the enemy. What, one wonders, do the extreme Muslin clerics offer the few women who have taken this extreme step: a line-up in paradise of Islamic studs?

But the suicide bombers are an irrelevance in my story of "conventional" suicide. In his book, Dr Joiner reveals that roughly one million people kill themselves each year: about one person every forty seconds. But these figures must be put into perspective. As a cause of death suicide hardly ranks statistically. Cancer and heart disease account for 52 per cent, compared with a little over one per cent for self destruction. Yet, as I can testify, when it happens in *your* family it is particularly cruel and shattering. And, as with us, it so often comes without warning. A recent study in the UK, called Suicide in Avon, found that 80 per cent of young men who had died by their own hand had had no contact with their doctor, psychiatrist or other support agency in the four months before their death. What's more, it seems that it can have a kind of contagious affect. As I write this, 21 young people living in or connected to the South Wales town of Bridgend in the UK have killed themselves in the last eighteen months by hanging. Police believe that they were not part of a suicide pact, but they can't unravel any link other than that of geography.

So what is a parent – a peripheral but not unimportant figure in this sad world of the suicide of young people – to deduce from the experience? What lessons to be learned to pass on to those who might find themselves potentially in the same situation?

Stay close. Whether you argue or acquiesce, whether you are firm or suppliant, stay close to your child. Studies of suicides have flagged up the signs of depression, summed up so firmly (if a touch clumsily, grammatically) by Dr Joiner, as: feelings of "burdensomeness and low belongingness." You will never know if these viruses are creeping into your child's brain unless you stay important to him. Of course, the relevance of parents to their child recedes in direct ratio to the child's age. To a young person in his/her late teen years, the influence of parents has usually diminished and been replaced by that of a peer group or a young lover. While recognising this, the wise parent will hang on in there, laying not too heavy nor too light a hand on the shoulder of his child, loving and caring to help him/her through the agonies. It may seem obvious and even trite advice, but I didn't follow it. For most families, it will be irrelevant. But to the tiny minority who might begin to glean some alarming behavioural clues in their child, it could prove vital.

Society's views on the act of suicide have changed. Aristotle judged that suicide was an act against the State, because on religious grounds it polluted the city and, economically, it weakened it by destroying a useful citizen. The Christian church, which found it completely acceptable in the form of martyrdom in the Roman arena, turned against it and, in 693 at the Council of Toledo, ordained that even attempted suicides should be excommunicated. In Britain, until 1870, the law ruled that a suicide's property would become the State's after his death and an unsuccessful suicide could be sent to prison – at least in theory – as late as 1961.

All of this, of course, was of no relevance at all to the person contemplating self-destruction. Boris Pasternak, in his "Essay on Autobiography," summed it all up and deserves the last (but one) word. He wrote: "a man who decides to commit suicide puts a full stop to his being; he turns his back to his past, he declares himself a bankrupt and his memories to be unreal. They can no longer help or save him, he has put himself beyond their reach. The continuity of his inner life is broken, his personality is at an end. And perhaps what finally makes him kill himself is not the firmness of his resolve but the unbearable quality of this anguish which belongs to no one, of this suffering in the absence of the sufferer, of this waiting which is empty because life has stopped and can no longer fill it…

"…What is certain is that they all suffered beyond description to the point where suffering has become a mental illness. And, as we bow in homage to their gifts and to their bright memory, we should bow compassionately before their suffering."

So there I must leave my son, glowing in my memory and of that of his mother and sister, and maybe still appearing – although inevitably less frequently – smiling and exuding exuberance in the recollections of those now middle-aged companions of his youth. To them and to us, of course, he can never grow old. It is one of the few consolations we have.

I must admit that the tragedy of Paul's loss has, in some ways provided a grim balance to the on the whole happy memories of my own childhood and of growing up in Birmingham during the war. But I would never, for one moment, have missed his company.

Some readers of this story may, perhaps, find that the two major and rather discrete parts of it – the tale of the boy growing up and the mature man probing into the death of his son – do not sit well together, despite the fact that I have stepped back into conventional autobiographical style by more briefly relating what happened in between.

If there must be a more iconic link, then let me leave the reader with these two images from the middle of the night: one of a young boy, curled up under the blankets in his bed in the early hours of the morning reading a book by torchlight while the rest of the house is asleep; and the other of a teenager many years later, perched on top of the stairs in a darkened house at the same witching hour, plucking up courage to hurl himself down the stairs to prove something or other. Both of them sons but one, alas, destined never to become a father.